About the Authors

Elizabeth Le Geyt was bird columnist for the Ottawa Citizen for 39 years. Dubbed the 'Bird Lady' by her readers, she retired in 2013 just three months before her 99th birthday. Born in Britain in 1914, Elizabeth has always been fascinated by the world of birds. After emigrating to Canada in 1952 with her young family, she continued

**ELIZABETH
LE GEYT**

her passion for birding by studying North American species. Elizabeth was named to the Order of Ontario in 2012 for her lifetime of activities in support of the environment; in 2013, she was awarded the Queen's Jubilee Medal.

Michael Le Geyt is Elizabeth's son. He recorded and transcribed her memoirs when arthritis of the hands prevented Elizabeth from writing them herself. Michael is a scientist with a doctorate from the University of British Columbia. He shares his mother's love for the natural world and is keenly interested in the native birds and wildflowers of British Columbia.

Bird Lady

A Lifelong Love Affair with Birds

....

BY ELIZABETH LE GEYT
WITH
MICHAEL LE GEYT

Photo Credits
Front Cover
Resplendent Quetzal, Saul Bocian
Back Cover
Atlantic Puffin, Tony Beck

Northern Cardinal and Rose-breasted Grosbeak,
Calvin D. Hanson

First Edition – May 2014

ISBN
978-1-4602-4259-9 (Hardcover)
978-1-4602-4260-5 (Paperback)
978-1-4602-4261-2 (eBook)

Produced by:

FriesenPress
Suite 300 – 852 Fort Street
Victoria, BC, Canada V8W 1H8

www.friesenpress.com

Distributed to the trade by The Ingram Book Company

Dedication:

This book is dedicated to all birdlovers and the
beautiful birds that have enriched my life.

Please be a vigilant protector
of the natural world and
its creatures.

Elizabeth Le Geyt

Michael Le Geyt

Table of Contents

Acknowledgements

. . . .

It is with profound gratitude that I acknowledge all those who have helped with the creation of this book, as well as all the birding enthusiasts who supplied me with sighting reports and photographs over my years as the bird columnist for the Ottawa *Citizen*. Without the support of so many wonderful individuals, neither the newspaper column nor this book would have been possible.

In particular, I would like to thank the management and staff at the Ottawa *Citizen* for the opportunity to write their bird column for 39 years. I am especially indebted to a succession of long-suffering editors who patiently dealt with my assorted computer misadventures. I would also like to thank the owners, management and staff at the Orchard View Living Centre who have provided me with every assistance for many years; the late Kathy Nihei and the management and staff of the Ottawa Valley Wild Bird Care Centre for their passion, commitment and expertise in the handling of injured and orphaned birds; the Ottawa Field-Naturalists' Club for assistance with sighting reports and for their environmental advocacy; Ray Holland for his friendship and support with the care of juvenile birds;

to my longtime computer guru, Harvey Hope, upon whom I relied greatly to keep my computer operational; and to Barbara Stinson, Malcolm McMillan and Linda Ryan, all of whom have faithfully refilled my birdfeeders for years.

I would also like to thank Linda Stanfield of Salt Spring Island, B.C. for her meticulous editing of the book manuscript. Any errors or omissions that remain are strictly the authors' responsibility. I also thank photographers Tony Beck, Saul Bocian, Bruce Di Labio, Judith Gustafsson, Calvin D. Hanson and John Le Geyt for making their superb images available for this book as well as on the website *birdladybook.com*, where their photographs may be viewed in colour.

Chapter 1:
MY EARLY YEARS IN BRITAIN

. . . .

I can never recall a time when I was not looking at birds: I suspect that I watched them when I was still in a pram. I was born in England in June of 1914, just a few months before the outbreak of the First Great War. My family lived in various places around London and finally settled on the outskirts of St. Albans, where I had my first memorable birding experience at the age of five. It was a puzzling sight — a tiny adult was feeding a huge baby! My mother explained to me that this baby was a cuckoo. The common cuckoo is a large, grey-speckled bird that calls out in a loud voice, *"cuck-oo, cuck-oo"*, a cry that is the first sign of an English spring.

The cuckoo is a parasite: it lays its eggs in other birds' nests and lets them raise its babies. The cuckoo in our garden had laid its egg in the nest of a hedge sparrow (which is not a true sparrow but a dunnock in the Accentor family). It is dark, stripy-brown and quite small; the cuckoo, on the other hand, is enormous. The cuckoo baby had left the nest and was learning to fly about in the garden. When I saw the fledgling, it was standing on the pathway shrieking for food. The microscopic hedge sparrow practically needed a ladder to feed this behemoth baby. When the cuckoo opened its huge, orange-red mouth, the tiny sparrow popped a morsel into it. I can see it now as clearly as on the day it happened, even though it was ninety-five years ago.

Early in my childhood we moved north to Little Hayward in Staffordshire where we lived beside a canal. My brother David and I loved that canal. We would buy a freshly baked loaf of bread from the little bakery behind our house, take a huge pat of butter and a pot of jam, and spend the afternoon on the canal. A kindly neighbour allowed us to use a small, flat-bottomed punt that he kept moored at his dock. To reach the dock we had to pass through his yard, which was patrolled by a gander that was very protective of its territory. This large bird would come up behind us, hissing loudly with neck outstretched, and stop only when its beak was nearly touching our bare calves — very unnerving.

A pair of mute swans had built a nest on one of the canal banks. The male swan was as protective of his nest as the gander was of his property. If we came too close, he would charge from his nest, feathers all fluffed up, with enough speed to create a bow wave. After he had shooed us away, he would then sail gracefully back to his mate and keep her company beside the nest.

On the sunny side of the canal, there were grand blackberries that we would add to our picnic tea. Whenever we saw a horse-drawn barge approaching, we would row our punt away from the towing bank in order to avoid it. Once we were caught by surprise with the speed and maneuverability of a motorized barge, a new-fangled invention at that time. We expected it to hug the bank with the towpath, but when it veered to the opposite bank at the same moment we did, we nearly collided.

We loved to walk our dogs up and down the towpath beside the canal. That was the only time in my life that I have seen a Eurasian kingfisher, one of the few highly coloured birds in Britain: perhaps the gloomy climate encourages birds to be drab so as to fit in. This kingfisher is a small bird, a glorious iridescent turquoise blue with a robin-red breast, white underparts and a rattling call. It is a clever bird, able to compensate for the refraction of the water's surface when diving, and nearly always successful. I was excited to watch the kingfisher's lightning plunge, the explosion of water and its emergence with a wriggling, silver minnow.

Our Sealyham terriers
Photo by Elizabeth Le Geyt

A love of the natural world ran deeply through my family. My grandfather, who was the coroner of Nottingham, established the arboretum in that city and even wrote a little nature book. Unfortunately, he was not able to pass on his extensive knowledge to his daughter (my mother) who remained

. . . .

convinced that Cock Robin and Jenny Wren were husband and wife. Despite her imperfect understanding of nature's ways, my mother did harbour an abiding love for the environment, a trait that she passed on to David and me. The fact that our family always lived in the countryside made it easier to pursue that interest.

We often visited a little pond close by our house. There we captured newts, tadpoles, frogs and turtles and took them home to our aquarium, where we looked after them and observed their daily activities. One summer we captured dragonfly larvae (called nymphs). They proved to be absolute devils — they ate virtually everything. As a result there wasn't much else in our aquarium that year. One day we were supposed to have a picnic lunch but it rained, and so the picnic was cancelled. Our initial disappointment soon turned to excitement when one of the nymphs climbed out of the water onto a reed to begin its meta-morphosis. We watched in fascination as its back split open, and the adult dragonfly struggled to climb out. At first its wings were all crumpled, but gradually they swelled to full size. What a vivid memory that was — the adult dragonfly slowly flexing its new wings while its empty larval case still clung to the reed!

I was living at Little Hayward when I first went away to attend boarding school at the age of twelve. When David and I returned home for the holidays, we would immediately go birding in the nearby hills and moors, which were covered in bracken, gorse and heather. There we would see birds like European stonechats, whinchats and common redstarts — very different from the great tits and blue tits that flitted around our home garden.

I graduated from boarding school at age seventeen and then returned to live with my parents. In my absence they had moved to Bothwell, Scotland, a town on the River Clyde in a coal-mining district just south of Glasgow. My father was an engineer and had been offered a senior position in a large iron and steel plant. One of my favourite sights around Bothwell was a heronry of nesting great blue herons. The herons were incredibly noisy as they perched on their absurdly small stick nests high in the trees. How on earth did those gawky young birds, seemingly all legs and beaks, not fall out of their flimsy nests?

A GREAT BLUE HERON NEST
PHOTO BY JUDITH GUSTAFSSON

It was on the frozen Clyde that I learned how to skate one winter. The ice was covered in black soot from all the industrial emissions of that era. As a novice skater I fell, and fell, and fell. By the time I returned home for lunch, I looked like a chimney sweep: my clothes, my face, my hair — they were all covered in soot. When the Clyde was not frozen, there were ducks galore, and slowly but steadily, I learned to identify them.

The move to Scotland provided more of a culture shock than we had anticipated. One day my mother and I decided to go bicycling as we had always done in England. It was the time of the Depression, and large knots of men were gathered along the roadways in the hope of picking up casual labour. The sight of two women cycling past caused the men to hoot and whistle loudly. We were so dismayed, even alarmed, that we never cycled again. My parents became increasingly dissatisfied with life in Bothwell. We relocated to the little market town of Strathaven, close to the heather moors, where there were Eurasian curlews and all kinds of other lovely things.

When I finished boarding school in 1933, I entered a teacher's college located in the Lake District and completed a two-year course that resulted in a teaching diploma. My mother had graduated from the same college thirty years earlier. Soon after graduation I was called into the college and told that I had been offered a position in a small elementary school located in Newcastle on the northeast coast of England. Ellen Bicknell was the headmistress in this school. I inquired which subjects I would be expected to teach and could hardly believe my ears when I heard the response: Latin, grammar and singing. I started to laugh for Latin and grammar were two of my worst subjects in school!

I was forced to cram each lesson in order to stay one step ahead of my pupils, who were aged six to twelve. We had some wonderful Latin texts that spoke about sailors being shipwrecked on islands with parrots and other unusual things — it was all so interesting. As time went by, the obvious connection between Latin and English grammar became apparent to me, and that made my life easier. Singing was more relaxed because I had always been involved with music. I was put in charge of the hymns that we had to sing each morning and evening, a responsibility that over the years led me to conclude that almost everyone can learn to sing. In my five years of teaching, I had only one child with perfect pitch and quickly made her a leader for the others to follow. I also had a child who droned like a bagpipe — she could hit just one note. Fortunately, she was the only such child I had in my teaching career.

When my teaching schedule allowed, I would often go with other birders on a ferry ride to the nearby Farne Islands, a group of 15 to 20 islands located off the Northumberland coast. We were frequently accompanied on these trips by Dr. T. Russell Goddard, Curator of the Newcastle Museum, a kind and gentle man who took pains to share his immense knowledge of the natural world with us. The Farnes are mostly low islands but marked with occasional rocky cliffs that were protected as a bird sanctuary due to the large numbers of nesting kittiwakes, gannets, shags, cormorants, puffins and terns. The low beaches of the islands were used extensively by the grey seals, which gave birth to their furry, white pups there each November.

ATLANTIC PUFFINS
PHOTO BY TONY BECK

NORTHERN GANNET
PHOTO BY TONY BECK

In the 1920s the islands were used by both birds and people. Visitors were cautioned not to descend into the ternery where the nests were so close together that it would be impossible not to walk on them. Even in those days, people with cameras wanted to get as close as possible to the birds in order to obtain the ultimate photograph. Signs implored visitors to remain behind a rope barrier. Those who ignored the signs usually wore protective headgear or carried a stick to fend off the terns, which were very aggressive. Despite the warning signs, one man was determined to go down for a better photograph. He had nothing on his head; indeed, he was completely bald. He was instantly spotted by a very angry tern intent on protecting its nest. Down swooped the tern and raked the man across the top of his head, tearing open a gash that promptly oozed a trickle of blood. The wounded man beat a hasty retreat. I thought this was terrific retribution for disregarding the warning.

Chapter 2:
THE SECOND GREAT WAR

. . . .

Shortly after World War II began, I accepted a marriage proposal from Jack Le Geyt, an officer in the Royal Navy. We were married in the county of Kent, located in the southeastern corner of England, in January of 1940. It was fiendishly cold with several feet of snow on the ground. We were married on a Saturday and had two days of honeymoon before Jack was required to return to naval service. During that time we acquired a dog and returned to the small cottage that we had rented. The lane was impassable, and our car became stuck in a snowdrift; luckily, we had a shovel. We were able to make a path to the cottage for ourselves, the dog, and his enormous bag of dog food. When we reached the cottage, we discovered that the pipes were frozen. We spent a frigid evening without heat, melting pots of snow that yielded a very small amount of very dirty water. My husband had purchased a double bed but it had not yet been delivered. We spent the night in a single bed with everything that we could find piled on top of us, including the dog and Jack's greatcoat. It was unreal. What an inauspicious start to a marriage!

We lived there in the little house, located dangerously close to Lympne Airbase on the outskirts of Folkestone, until the following summer when the coastal towns of Britain came under regular attack. The Royal Navy was stationed at the airbase when the German Army overran France, forcing the miraculous evacuation of British and Allied troops at Dunkirk. The military High Command abruptly decided that Lympne Airbase was urgently required for the Royal Air Force: the Navy was given 24 hours to vacate. Naval officers and sailors were hurriedly relocated to Newcastle-under-Lyme in the midlands, leaving the wives to pack up and follow. Alone on the night following the men's departure, I experienced my first air raid siren alert. I was very frightened. I collected the dog and ran next door to shelter with my neighbour, an army wife; we were both relieved when there was no attack. Thereafter I too moved to Newcastle-under-Lyme where we lived for only a few months before Jack was ordered to sea for an extended period. I was feeling very low at this time. I was befriended by a local lady who assured me that the cure for depression was to buy a new hat! To my consternation I also discovered that I was pregnant, despite our plan not to have children until after the war. I decided to go home to live with my parents in Scotland.

Because of its distance from Germany, Glasgow had only two air raids in the entire war. One raid took place on the night of March 13, 1941. I remember that date well because my first child was due, and I was expecting to go into labour at any moment. We were up all night as the German planes came in, wave after wave. The sky was a hive of activity with bombers continuously buzzing overhead. One of the bombers dropped its load in a nearby field. The next morning we went out to inspect the string of craters left behind; fortunately, that was as close as any bomb came to me during the war. I gave birth the following day in my parents' home with the assistance of an excellent midwife named Amy, who stayed with me for the following three weeks. After a surprisingly easy six hours of labour, a healthy baby boy emerged into the world early on the morning of March 15th. We named him John.

We used to get our milk delivered by the young children of the dairy farmer who lived next door to us. Shortly after John entered the world, a boy and girl, aged about five and four respectively, showed up at the front door with our daily quota of milk. We thought that they might like to see the new baby and so invited them in to meet John. The little boy looked up at me wide-eyed and asked, "Did God bring him?" Before I could respond, his younger sister interjected confidently, "No silly, the doctor brought him in his black bag." I thought that was just wonderful.

With the war and the arrival of John, I did very little active birding. My parents always maintained a beautiful garden so we were constantly visited by birds, including one of my favourites, the European robin, a darling little bird. We used to hang up coconut shells that had been split open to expose the white fleshy meat. Later we learned that feeding coconut was ill advised: several blue tits had been found dead with their stomachs full of undigested coconut. That was a useful learning experience about the importance of providing appropriate foods to birds.

Living in someone else's home is not easy, especially when that person is a mother who tends to fuss and criticize. I opted to leave Scotland and rent quarters from the brother of Ellen Bicknell. I did not find it much easier there — I was pregnant again — and John was two years old, a most challenging age. My second pregnancy was difficult. My doctor was constantly in demand to treat war-related injuries. I practically had to grab him by the coattails to get his attention. When I went into labour in February of 1943, it was cold, dark, and typically, in the middle of the night. I was admitted to the local nursing home, which was absolutely freezing, even when I was in bed. I asked for a hot water bottle but was refused; instead, the nurse turned off the light and left the room. What a difference from my experience with my trusted midwife, Amy, who had stayed with me, talked to me and rubbed my back. The painful labour continued and then stalled as the baby became lodged in the birth canal, necessitating a high forceps delivery. Finally, battered and bruised, another baby boy entered the world. We named him Christopher.

Jack came home on leave when Christopher was born. With a growing family we moved again to a larger home where we stayed for the remainder of the war. Our rental agreement came with two stipulations: we were to wind the enormous clock collection once a week; and we were not to take down any of the paintings (which ranged from ghastly to hideous). Before the end of the war I was pregnant once more, and once more, a baby boy entered the world: Ashley had arrived.

When Jack was stationed in Plymouth at the end of World War II, our family relocated to the westcountry county of Devon. Our new home was in a beautiful rural setting south of Tavistock, overlooking a lovely valley on the edge of Dartmoor. We had a number of birds that came into the garden regularly, especially blue tits — lively small birds closely related to chickadees. We started a vegetable garden but were stymied by a small creature gnawing at the seedlings. I promptly set out a mousetrap to capture the offending pest. Imagine my consternation when I went out in the morning to discover a dead blue tit inside the trap. It was most distressing and made me realize that one must be very careful in the placement of animal traps.

Time passed and I gave birth to our fourth son. We named him Michael. We spent four more delightful years in Devon before the day that I received a phone call from my husband in Plymouth.

"Are you sitting down?" he inquired.

"Yes," I replied.

"Do you have seasickness pills?" he continued.

"Why would I need them?" I asked, puzzled.

"Because we're going to Canada," came the unexpected reply.

Chapter 3:
ADJUSTING TO LIFE IN CANADA

To say that I was surprised by my husband's sudden pronouncement is putting it mildly — I was stunned! I would be leaving my family, my friends and all my support systems to live in a strange, cold country. In November of 1952 Jack and I set sail from Liverpool aboard the RMS *Empress of Canada* bound for Saint John, New Brunswick. We were accompanied by our four children and 26 pieces of the most atrocious baggage — dilapidated suitcases, holdalls and tin trunks. We travelled first class thanks to the Royal Navy, which was 'loaning' Jack for a senior engineering position in the Canadian Navy. It would be the last westbound voyage for that ship, which caught fire in Liverpool Harbour on the return leg; the damage was so severe that the ship had to be scrapped.

Upon disembarking at the Customs and Immigration hall in Saint John, we learned that we were the first arrivals in a brand new facility. The brass were present for the inauguration, and the staff were especially punctilious that day. Despite the presence of four tired and restless little boys — aged four, six, eight and ten — and our impressive pile of decrepit baggage, the staff decided that it would be necessary to inspect every piece for contraband. The poor customs officer began to wade through all our belongings, shuffling through teddy bears, rooting through pyjamas and tossing aside all the usual trappings of a young and growing family. Soon the officer came to the two largest trunks, which had been corded for added strength. He cast a quick glance to the far end of the warehouse where his superior was working and then mercifully marked them both with an 'X' to indicate that they had been inspected. The news media were present that day to record the opening of the new facility. They requested that the four boys perch on top of our enormous pile of baggage, and a photo was taken. The picture appeared in print the following day, alongside a picture of a very respectable group of well-dressed individuals; unfortunately, the captions were reversed!

We spent the day in Saint John waiting for the night train to Halifax, Nova Scotia, where Jack's new position was based. There were bunks everywhere in the roomette, up and down on both sides, as well as under the window. It was terribly cramped for six people: I felt positively claustrophobic. When we reached Halifax, we checked into a hotel where the main space for the children to play was the front lobby. I spent most of my time preventing our little boys from running around and making a great racket in the public rooms. Jack reckoned that it would be fine to stay at the hotel until after Christmas — more than a month away! He had been at sea for so much of our marriage that he really had no idea what family life was all about, especially with four young boys gadding about. One day he went out shopping for a car with our limited resources so that we could be mobile. Imagine my surprise when he returned to announce that he had purchased a house!

So it was that we moved into a tiny dwelling in Armdale, then an outlying district of Halifax. We had no household effects like furniture or beds, and no kitchen necessities like cutlery or plates. The only items we had to put in the house were four little boys and our pile of baggage. Thankfully the Navy was used to this type of household move and stepped in efficiently to provide us with a refrigerator, a table and chairs, and beds. Jack purchased a solid mahogany bedroom suite, and little by little, we became established. We met our first Canadians — the Clarks, also a naval family — who became lifelong friends.

Our new home was a split-level with the kitchen located above the garage. From the kitchen window I looked directly into a large leafy tree where I watched for the strange new birds passing through the garden. I was flummoxed by my very first sighting. According to my field guide it was a female American redstart belonging to the Warbler family. This confused me for the Old World common redstart is a much larger, insectivorous, ground-feeding bird. It was my first learning experience about the problem of identical common names applied to quite different species. The same problem exists with the robin: the Old World European robin is quite small and classified as a chat, while the New World American robin is much larger and is classified as a thrush. I was very pleased the day that I was able to identify a yellow-billed cuckoo, the less common of the two North American cuckoo species.

My most exciting new discovery occurred the day that I was down on my hands and knees, scrubbing the flagstones at the entrance to our home. A small patch of red nasturtiums was in bloom to one side of these flagstones. Suddenly right beside my head and whirring in my ear was my first hummingbird, a male ruby-throated. I couldn't believe the antics of this little bird with the flashing red throat. It was really quite astonishing! The hummingbird is a species found only in the Americas so I had never seen one in Britain.

· ·

RUBY-THROATED HUMMINGBIRD (MALE)
PHOTO BY CALVIN D. HANSON

Early in 1955 I learned that I was pregnant again. I decided
to return to Britain, visit with my parents and give birth there.
Yet another son arrived in October, making a grand total of five
boys: we named the new arrival Philip. I returned with my baby
via ship to New York City in January of 1956. Winter cross-
ings of the North Atlantic are frequently rough at the best of
times. On this voyage our crossing was made even worse by
the tail end of a hurricane. After reaching New York in a rather
ragged condition, Philip and I boarded a train for Ottawa. In my

absence Jack had relocated there with our family after receiving a transfer from the Canadian Navy.

No sooner had I returned than Jack suggested yet another move, this time to the countryside. We discovered a small house along the banks of the Rideau River just south of Manotick. It was a rural property owned by the local Catholic priest, Father Finn. He was a bit of an entrepreneur who had already built and sold several houses. We were fortunate to find this one before it was listed. The good father was quite pleased when a young Catholic family appeared on the scene, and he gave us a moderately good deal on the purchase.

Chapter 4:
BIRDING IN THE OTTAWA REGION

Birding in the Ottawa region takes place throughout eastern Ontario between the Ottawa and St. Lawrence rivers and northward into the Gatineau Hills of Quebec. Blessed with a wide variety of habitat — rivers, lakes, marshes, farms, fields and forests — the area is attractive to many species of birds. Raptors, shorebirds, woodpeckers, swallows, sparrows and songbirds are attracted to different areas of this diverse habitat. They are joined in springtime by a myriad of migrants that spread out to nest and raise their families. Some of these visitors are our most vividly coloured birds — Baltimore orioles, rose-breasted grosbeaks, indigo buntings, scarlet tanagers and ruby-throated hummingbirds. Colourful warblers, those tiny hyperactive jewels that flit about in the woods, also arrive in springtime; more than 30 species have been recorded. The difficulty of identifying these warblers and learning their songs presents a constant challenge for birders. More challenging still, even for the most experienced birders, are their relatively nondescript offspring, aptly described in field guides as 'Confusing Fall Warblers'.

The Ottawa region is fortunate to be located along a principal migration flyway: it extends from the Arctic to the eastern seaboard of the United States and then onward to Central and South America, where many of our birds overwinter. Even tiny hummingbirds undertake this long, hazardous journey, crossing the Gulf of Mexico along the way. Scientists and birders have long been intrigued by the migration of birds. Why do they do it? Why do they travel so far? How do they find their way? Year after year they seek out summer homes in the north and then go back to their winter homes in the south.

While the juveniles of many species fly with their parents to learn the migration route, there are some, such as shorebirds, that undertake migration on their own. Many shorebirds choose to breed and nest in the Arctic tundra. Parents will typically depart for southern climes well before their offspring are ready for the lengthy flight. Their half-grown, precocial youngsters are left to fend for themselves. These chicks complete their development and then respond to the migration instinct to fly south; some even catch up to their slower-moving parents. When water levels are low, birders can occasionally observe both adults and offspring feeding together on the mudflats of the Ottawa River and nearby lagoons. The intermingling of young and adult shorebird species, some of which are now sporting their winter plumage, presents as great a challenge to birders as do the 'Confusing Fall Warblers'.

The Britannia Conservation Area, with Mud Lake and its surrounding deciduous forest, is one of the best year-round birding areas in the Ottawa region. Black-crowned night herons have settled into the Conservation Area and are breeding successfully — they are now a common sight for birders. While most migrating warblers and vireos pass through the Ottawa region, some remain and nest in the woods at Britannia. Female Baltimore orioles can sometimes be seen weaving their intricate ball nests in the forest canopy, while great horned owls do little more than settle onto a broken snag or disused raptor nest to raise their young.

The Ottawa River, which forms a large part of the interprovincial boundary between Ontario and Quebec, empties into the St. Lawrence River at Montreal. Sections of the river, especially around Shirley's Bay, provide diverse habitat for many bird species. In the middle of the Deschênes Rapids, there is a small island with a large number of mature trees. Protected by the turbulent waters of the rapids, the island is not easily accessible to humans. It has long been a favoured nesting place for great blue herons and more recently, double-crested cormorants and great egrets. The egrets first nested here in 2011, a fact that was confirmed in 2012 when fledglings were observed. More and more egrets are being seen every year. Bald eagles, still recovering from the disastrous DDT era, nested successfully at nearby Shirley's Bay in 2011 and again in 2012.

BALD EAGLE
PHOTO BY JUDITH GUSTAFSSON

Also located in the Ottawa River, downstream from the city, is Petrie Island, a shoal of sand and clay deposited at the end of the last Ice Age. The shoal consists of one large island and many smaller ones, with the whole collection known as Petrie Island. The island has an Interpretive Centre, nature trails, a wooded area, and several marshy ponds. There are beaches and sandy picnic areas in Stuemer Park. The Province of Ontario has recognized Petrie Island as 'an area of natural and scientific interest' and designated it as 'Significant Wetland'. It contains the only known Carolinian swamp forest located north of Toronto and is home to the unusual hackberry tree. More than 130 bird species have been recorded on Petrie Island; the extremely rich habitat also supports several species of turtle, some of which are rare.

There are many other protected green spaces along the banks of the Ottawa River, as well as on the banks of its tributary, the Rideau River. Andrew Haydon Park, Vincent Massey Park and Hog's Back Park are all good-sized parks that support significant birdlife.

The Mer Bleue Conservation Area, located east of Ottawa, was once slated to be drained but was saved from this fate by the concerted efforts of environmentalists. This ancient bog provides habitat for many species of uncommon plants and birds that are more typically found in northern boreal bogs. The Mer Bleue is also a staging area for fall-migrating red-winged blackbirds, which assemble in countless thousands. Sandhill cranes have nested here for many years. Large numbers of these dancing cranes have a preferred migratory stop, both coming and going, in nearby Navan.

The Central Experimental Farm, established as a farming research centre by the federal Department of Agriculture in 1886, occupies a wide swath of green space in the heart of Ottawa. The open spaces and extensive fields attract raptors, which enjoy freedom of movement and good hunting territory. Piles of manure draw many species of migratory birds. It was here that I saw my first Lapland longspur: it is one of our earliest arriving migrants, often travelling in the company of horned larks.

I recommend visiting the nearby Fletcher Wildlife Garden, which is located at the edge of the Farm. It is a demonstration garden that shows visitors how to create or restore wildlife-friendly gardens through good design and appropriate plantings. Many species of birds have nested in this wildlife sanctuary over the years, including a pair of green herons; local photographers keenly recorded them building their nests and raising their families. Also adjacent to the Central Experimental Farm is the Dominion Arboretum, which was founded in 1889 with plantings of trees from all over the world. A benevolent microclimate — one zone warmer than the rest of Ottawa — has allowed uncommon trees, such as magnolias, azaleas, *Sequoiadendron* and *Liriodendron*, to survive to maturity. The Arboretum also contains a large collection of crabapples trees, which burst into a profusion of pink-shaded blossoms in spring.

The city of Ottawa is surrounded by a crescent of lightly developed land known as the Greenbelt. A mix of forest, wetlands, farms and fields, the Greenbelt serves as another relatively safe area for the region's wild creatures. Just outside the Greenbelt in a southwesterly direction from the city, the Trail Road Landfill Site attracts great flocks of gulls — herring, ring-billed, great black-backed, lesser black-backed, glaucous and Iceland species, amongst others. Both adult and juvenile gulls can be observed there in all their complex plumages.

Along nearby Moodie Drive, waterfowl have discovered a large pond; it can be viewed from the road and is worth investigating to see what new arrivals have appeared. The Wild Bird Care Centre is located to the north of this pond at 734 Moodie

Drive. The Jackpine Trail is also located along Moodie Drive in an area known as Stony Swamp. This area is particularly rewarding for birders in winter when its public feeders attract chickadees, nuthatches and woodpeckers. All of these birds can be fed by hand with oiled sunflower seeds, a most rewarding activity for families with children. Another trail at Stony Swamp leads to a marshy area where herons and rails can often be seen in summertime.

Eastern bluebirds are one of my most favourite birds, especially the males with their lovely blue and chestnut colouration and captivating song. For many years bluebirds nested in natural tree cavities and within holes in cedar rail fences. From their nests they would forage for insects in the open pasture fields grazed by cattle. Over time habitat suitable for bluebirds has steadily diminished. Fortunately, humans have come to the rescue with specially designed bluebird trails and nestboxes. This endeavour has proved to be very successful, with the result that most bluebirds around Ottawa are now found along these trails.

The Ottawa region has long been fortunate to have many organizations devoted to protecting its rich environment. Volunteer groups, such as field-naturalist clubs, natural history societies, nature conservancies, riverkeepers and the like, have donated countless hours to preserve and protect habitat as well as the many creatures that dwell therein. Two such dedicated volunteers are long-time residents Brian and June Pye. They were pioneers in establishing an important bluebird trail along the Armstrong and Bowesville roads, just south of the Ottawa airport. It has been a great success and has flourished for many years, but encroachment from road building and housing construction threatens its survival.

Competition for nestboxes laid out along the Pyes' bluebird trail has always been fierce. Tree swallows regularly take over many of the boxes, which is not a bad thing, as they too are in decline. In 2013 the Pyes reported that many bluebirds nested and successfully raised their first brood. Unfortunately for the bluebirds, many of their nestboxes were then taken over by wrens, forcing the evicted bluebirds to look elsewhere to raise their second brood. There are other nuisances too. Vandals frequently destroy boxes, leaving shattered remnants strewn on the ground, while other boxes are simply stolen. Despite these complications the summer of 2013 was a good year for the bluebirds. In early fall a flock of 26 adults and juveniles was seen gathered near the trail, a wonderful testimonial to the efforts of the Pyes.

The Pyes also care for purple martins, large members of the Swallow family that like to nest communally. Years ago Brian Pye built a martin house, an 'apartment nestbox' with multiple cavities. The martins immediately filled it to capacity and raised many broods of fledglings. Despite the declining population of swallows, the Pyes' martin house has remained faithfully full over the years.

Peter Huszcz, a mechanic and inventor, is another tireless volunteer. As a bird lover he has devoted his considerable talents to assisting bluebirds, purple martins and osprey. Peter installed a nesting platform for osprey along the Ottawa River. It remained unused for several years but was recently occupied by a pair of osprey, which nested successfully. Peter also designed, constructed and installed two purple martin houses at the Nepean Sailing Club. Both houses were filled to capacity in the first year that they were put in place. Peter's goal was to achieve a total of 300 fledglings. Remarkably, he fell just two short of that objective with a grand total of 298 young birds. In the following year the number of young birds dipped to fewer than 200, due in part to a prolonged cold, wet spring. A further decline was seen the year after when the weather pattern re-appeared, reducing the population of flying insects. Insufficient food for the adult birds in early spring can diminish their reproductive capacity. Peter has also established a martin colony with two houses in his home garden. With the aid of an audio recording of purple martins calling to each other, he was able to attract six breeding pairs in the first year. In subsequent years the martin population at his boxes has grown steadily.

A MARTIN HOUSE
PHOTO BY PETER HUSZCZ

PETER HUSZCZ AND ELIZABETH

Peter has a bird-banding licence, which allows him to band all his juvenile martins before they become free-flying. To acquire such a licence requires specialized skill and knowledge gained over many years, usually under the supervision of an experienced, licenced bander. Licences are issued by the Bird Banding Office of Environment Canada under the authority of the *Migratory Birds Convention Act.*

Peter has generously allowed visitors to observe his banding at the Nepean Sailing Club. This is an excellent opportunity for families with children to see these magnificent birds up close and learn more about their role in the environment. Peter is a very large man with very large hands. To watch him handle the fledgling birds with such skill and aplomb is truly a sight to behold. Look for newspaper announcements about the dates and times of Peter's banding demonstrations.

Chapter 5:
LIVING BESIDE THE RIDEAU RIVER

....

Our new house was located on the east bank of the Rideau River just south of the village of Manotick. It was little more than a glorified cottage with four tiny bedrooms. The waterfront lot on which it stood looked south down the river, which widened into a large bay in front of our property. When the river rose during the spring melt, a powerful circular current swept around this bay. The day that the bay ice broke up was eagerly anticipated. Each year we would place our names on the calendar to guess the correct date. The small house stood in the middle of an empty field with just a single, young elm tree and a shrubby dogwood growing at the water's edge. We immediately planted trees — weedy but fast-growing weeping willows, Chinese elms and Lombardy poplars — as the bones of our new garden.

OUR HOUSE AT MANOTICK
PHOTO BY ELIZABETH LE GEYT

Birdwatching became a daily activity as soon as I placed feeding stations around the garden. A small crabapple tree delighted us with its drifts of pink blossoms in spring. I was even more pleased when its frozen burgundy fruits attracted a flock of beautiful pine grosbeaks during the following winter. The males, a lovely crimson and grey, were surprisingly tame. They were quite content to continue feeding even when we walked nearby. Evening grosbeaks, with their brilliant plumage of yellow, black and white, are close relatives of pine grosbeaks. During the 1950s and 1960s, great numbers of them came to the winter feeders. My largest feeding station was a picnic table fitted with a raised cover and trim around the edges to contain all the shells of the assorted birdseed. Large, striped sunflower seeds were the favourite food of the evening grosbeaks. So numerous were these birds that at times as many as 70 individuals jostled for position on the table. I marvelled how their perfectly adapted beaks extracted the sunflower seeds while the two shell casings flew in opposite directions. It became a daily ritual to sweep up the shell debris, which often accumulated to a depth of two centimeters on the table.

THE ANNUAL ICE BREAKUP WAS KEENLY ANTICIPATED.
Photo by Elizabeth Le Geyt

EVENING GROSBEAKS FEEDING
PHOTO BY HUGH PETRIE

I especially recall the day that a lone pine siskin was feeding in the centre of a large group of noisy and quarrelsome evening grosbeaks. The pine siskin is a very small member of the Finch family, stripy-brown with yellow in its wings and at the base of its tail. It is a tame, friendly bird and remarkably feisty for its size — this individual had no difficulty maintaining its position amongst its boisterous neighbours. Other finches that came to the feeder during the winter included common redpolls and purple finches. The redpolls were irregular visitors, their appearance depending on the adequacy of the conifer seed crop in the northern boreal forest. These lively pink and grey birds with red-topped heads could appear in large irruptions when that crop was insufficient. A closely related redpoll species, the hoary redpoll, was an occasional visitor along with the common redpolls. The hoary redpoll resembles a common redpoll covered in hoar frost. Purple finches were regular winter visitors as were pine siskins.

Over the years evening grosbeaks became less and less common at winter feeding stations in the Ottawa area — they are now rarely seen. Pockets of them remain, however, in some outlying areas like the Larose Forest. While the grosbeaks were filtering away, other birds, such as northern cardinals and red-bellied woodpeckers, began drifting up from the south. The cardinals are now well-established permanent residents and can be seen at feeders year-round. I was thrilled when the first ones appeared at a feeding station in my garden. They tended to visit very early in the morning or very late in the day, perhaps because these low light conditions helped to obscure their brilliant colours from potential predators. Male cardinals can become baffled by their own window reflections, which they battle furiously thinking that a rival has intruded into their territory. Their futile attempts to repel the phantom — pounding their reflections hour after hour, day after day — can drive a homeowner mad!

The ebb and flow of bird populations, especially at the edges of their ranges, occurs constantly in the natural world. Food supply, habitat loss, competition from other species, pesticides, and increasingly, climate change, are all contributing factors. When DDT was widely used, the raptor population — hawks, eagles and osprey for example — plummeted because the pesticide weakened the shells of their eggs. Since the DDT ban in North America (sadly, it is still widely used elsewhere in the world), raptor populations have rebounded. Osprey and bald eagles have done especially well, as have two bird-eating hawks, the Cooper's and sharp-shinned, which have learned that feeding stations provide a reliable source of prey. It can be distressing for a birder to see a favourite bird suddenly picked off by one of these marauding hawks, but of course that is all part of the balance of nature.

A MALE NORTHERN CARDINAL
PHOTO BY CALVIN D. HANSON

Winter occasionally brings down even more raptors from the north, especially when the local populations of mice, voles and lemmings plummet. Irruptions of great grey owls, hawk owls and snowy owls are regular, if infrequent, occurrences that are guaranteed to thrill birders. In our rural setting, surrounded by farms and woodlands, we caught occasional glimpses of these Arctic visitors. The sighting that I remember best was of a great grey owl. This is a tall bird, mottled with flecks of brown and grey; it has a black chin spot bordered by a mustache of white whiskers. Although this owl is longer than the great horned owl, it actually weighs much less. As a resident of the Arctic, it requires far more feathering to retain its body heat. Its size and preference to sit on top of a tall tree make it especially conspicuous during its occasional visits to the south.

The great grey owl has exceptional hearing and hunts only by sound. The first time that I saw one of these magnificent creatures, it was perched atop a tall pine tree. I was driving at the time and quickly pulled over to the side of the road. Suddenly the owl swooped down from its perch, maneuvered slightly as it approached the ground, and then plunged its talons deep into the snow, emerging with a wriggling mouse. It had been listening from that great distance and had not only pinpointed the precise location of its prey but had also captured it. A moment later, as the owl sat half buried in the snow, it swallowed the struggling mouse whole.

Snowy owls, gloriously white with flecks of black and luminous yellow eyes, are especially popular with birders when they put in their infrequent appearance. They have their preferred perches, especially fence posts, to which they return time and again. When such a perch has been identified, it is usually possible for a birder to find the owl in the same vicinity on subsequent visits. In the winters of 2011 and 2012, there were large irruptions of snowy owls across Canada and extending deep into the central United States, where their highly unusual appearance created a sensation. So intense was the interest that traffic jams of birders clogged the roadsides to observe them.

When the winter snows melted away and the leaves began to unfurl, one of my favourite activities was to go birdwatching down a nearby country lane. I would always take the dogs along; often, one of my sons would accompany me. Bordered on both sides by a strip of hardwood forest, this lane extended deep into uninhabited, rolling countryside through a patchwork of crops, fallow fields, woodland lots, bogs and other marshy terrain. Some of the woodland lots were coniferous, while others were hardwood forests of maple, ash, oak and beech. In springtime lovely wildflowers — red and white trilliums, yellow and purple violets, trout lilies and jack-in-the-pulpits — sparkled on the forest floor, offset by the cool, brilliant green of unfolding fern fronds. While the dogs wore themselves out hunting for mice, voles, chipmunks, squirrels and rabbits, the birdwatchers were able to seek out the many different bird species attracted by the mixed habitat and peaceful surroundings. The boundless mosquito population during the spring migration was sought out by many insect-eating species, including warblers, vireos, flycatchers and swallows.

SNOWY OWL ON FENCE POST
PHOTO BY BRUCE DI LABIO

SNOWY OWL IN FLIGHT
PHOTO BY BRUCE DI LABIO

The quiet woodlands appealed to some of our more secretive species, such as wrens, thrushes, rose-breasted grosbeaks, American woodcocks and owls. The wild marshes, with their occasional small ponds, attracted ducks, green and great blue herons, shorebirds, red-winged blackbirds and raptors. Fallow fields, which produced plentiful seedheads of thistle, Queen Anne's lace, mullein and aster, drew in American goldfinches, eastern meadowlarks, bobolinks, sparrows, and in winter, snow buntings. The milkweed growing among these plants supported a healthy population of orange and black monarch butterflies whose caterpillars fed on its leaves. The richness and diversity of habitat ensured that a walk down this splendid country lane would be a rewarding birding experience in any season.

I dubbed one special patch of woodland 'The Ovenbird Forest' for it was there that in times past I could be sure to find these charming, terrestrial wood warblers. Ovenbirds earn their curious name from the fact that they build a leaf-covered, domed nest (the 'oven') in which to lay their eggs. Unfortunately, they build this nest on the ground where their chicks are susceptible to predation by chipmunks. Male and female ovenbirds are similar: they have chunky bodies with long, pinkish legs, olive-green backs and white breasts streaked with black. An orange stripe on their crowns is flanked by stripes of black. Perhaps the most striking trait of this bird is its insistent call, "*teach-er, teach-er, teach-er*", which it trills repeatedly throughout the day as it forages. In my early years in Manotick, as many as four ovenbird pairs nested in this patch of forest. Gradually their numbers dwindled from four pairs to three, to two, and then to one; finally, they disappeared entirely for reasons unknown but in keeping with the global decline in bird populations. I am saddened by the loss of these unique birds and miss their welcoming call, which used to enliven 'The Ovenbird Forest'.

Over the years our collection of weedy garden trees grew quickly larger, thereby offering greater protection to the visiting birdlife. We put up boxes for the tree swallows, but these were very attractive to the many house sparrows. To prevent the sparrows from seizing a nestbox before the arrival of the migrating swallows, I would put a stick in the nestbox hole. When the swallows arrived, I would remove the stick and hope that they would be able to defend their nestbox against the opportunistic and aggressive sparrows. I stashed a small collection of pebbles on windowsills and doorsteps to help me ward off the sparrows and assist the swallows, which I much preferred. It was an ongoing battle each spring. Sometimes I was successful, sometimes not.

Our garage, which was attached to the house, was used for the storage of bicycles, construction materials, automobile tires and the like. Its door was never closed, allowing easy access for barn swallows, which nested in the rafters year after year. One year red squirrels chose to nest in the garage as well. Regrettably, that was also the year that a rat put in an appearance. The mother squirrel was fearful of the predatory new arrival. On a Sunday afternoon, as I was relaxing in a lawn chair in the garden, I witnessed her remove all her offspring. One by one she carried each limp baby, four in all, by the scruff of its neck across the lawn, under the fence, and up onto the roof of the neighbouring house where she had an alternative den.

Not all birds were successful in their efforts to nest in our garden. A pair of northern flickers once opted to build a nest inside the tall pole that supported the far end of my washing line. The two adult birds laboured for days to excavate a hole suitable to raise a family. No sooner had they completed their toil than it was taken over by a pair of aggressive European starlings. In typical starling fashion, they called upon their extended family for support and ganged up on the overwhelmed woodpecker couple. The loss of the flickers was very disappointing.

A number of other bird species did manage to nest successfully in our garden. Song sparrows regularly built their nests in a low bush at the corner of the vegetable garden and raised a brood each year. Chipping sparrows nested from time to time, usually choosing to build inside the rather thick Chinese elm hedge. One summer while I was clipping this hedge, I accidentally uncovered one of their nests. I quickly stuffed some of the branch clippings back into the hedge to cover up the nest, and the nestlings continued to develop and fledge normally.

American robins nested in various places throughout the garden, often in the most stupid places. They would surreptitiously build their nests and then scream loudly if anyone came close, thereby revealing exactly where they had built. Despite their prolific success, they really are quite a simple-minded bird. As I think back to the number of fledglings that were born into our Manotick garden, it gives me great pleasure to think how many survived to adulthood.

Chapter 6:
RAISING FLEDGLING BIRDS

....

Kathy Nihei, founder of the Wild Bird Care Centre, had always been interested in rescuing orphaned and injured wild birds. Her initial experience occurred late one fall when she saved a fledgling ruby-throated hummingbird, which was far too immature to join in the migration south. Kathy's only choice was to overwinter it inside her house. The hummingbird quickly established its favourite flight pathways, constantly visiting the feeders and perches that Kathy set out. When spring arrived, she released the young bird into the wild. This successful venture piqued Kathy's desire to continue helping birds in need. She began to accept orphaned and injured birds, which she cared for in the basement of her home. Following a complaint from neighbours, Kathy was forced to seek a new location for her rescue activities. She sought support from local government and was offered a forested plot of land within the National Capital Commission's Greenbelt. With volunteer labour and donated building materials, Kathy supervised the construction and development of the Wild Bird Care Centre (later renamed the Ottawa Valley Wild Bird Care Centre).

KATHY NIHEI

Kathy had a remarkable rapport with birds; she seemed telepathically connected to them. Most of the birds brought to the Centre were traumatized and upset, which made them difficult for staff to handle. As soon as Kathy arrived, a bird would calm down. I recall one occasion inside the owl cage at the rear of the Centre. Owls are especially averse to human intervention, and great horned owls in particular, with their powerful beaks and talons, present a serious hazard for staff. One such owl had been brought to the Centre that very morning and was still behaving aggressively. Kathy entered the walk-in cage and approached the owl, speaking quietly in soothing tones. Within five minutes the injured bird had relaxed and was even presenting its head to her for stroking. Kathy's passion for birds extended even to those that many people consider a nuisance — starlings, crows and pigeons. She believed that every bird had its place and insisted on treating them all, a conviction that often drew criticism. Kathy went to extraordinary lengths to rescue birds; once she even descended into a sewer to rescue some baby ducklings that had fallen through a grate!

When I was the Ottawa *Citizen*'s bird columnist, I was regularly contacted by people seeking advice about injured and orphaned birds. I would always refer these callers to the Wild Bird Care Centre. I became a frequent visitor to the Centre, resulting in a deep and lasting friendship with its founder. When Kathy began operations at the Centre, she assumed that she would be able to release juvenile and recovered birds directly into the surrounding forest. In the wild, parent birds continue to feed their offspring for some time after they leave the nest. Kathy expected to do likewise with her birds until they were successfully weaned, but government bureaucrats saw the situation differently. They decreed that the birds could not be released in the vicinity because there would be too many of them in one location. Furthermore, bird releases would supposedly interfere with an insect study being conducted by Carleton University researchers.

Kathy cast around for alternative solutions to this dilemma and asked if I would accept her fledgling American robins for release. Baby robins are the most commonly rescued bird in nesting season because they tend to leave their nest before being fully fledged and are then 'rescued' by well-meaning humans. That was how I began to assist Kathy. When the robins were ready for release, they came to me. With its varied habitat, my rural setting was well suited for this purpose. My participation was strictly illegal for I did not have a permit, but I doubt at my advanced age that I shall be prosecuted for this admission.

Initially most of my releases were robins from the Centre, combined with the odd bird that was dropped off at my home by a concerned individual. Most of these delivered 'robins' turned out to be European starlings, but I cared for them anyway. When I received birds for release, I would first keep them indoors and place them in cages in my large sun porch. The house would suddenly become a cacophony of chirping baby birds, which had to be fed every hour on the hour from dawn until dusk. Outside I had a number of ground cages, which served as a transition home for the fledglings. There they could look into the garden and become accustomed to the great world beyond. My son John built a large aviary at one end of the sun porch, a permanent structure in which juvenile birds could make short flights and perfect their landing techniques.

I used this aviary more frequently after 'The Bullfrog Incident'. Shortly after I had placed some young robins in a ground cage, I looked out and saw, with great pleasure, a large bullfrog on my lawn. "Isn't that nice?" I thought. Later in the day when I glanced out, I saw to my surprise that the bullfrog was leaping at the ground cage in an attempt to get at the robins. I returned to the house and consulted one of my nature reference books. When I turned to the section that described bullfrogs, I was taken aback to see an illustration of a bullfrog devouring a baby robin! I thought to myself, "Well, you're not as welcome as I thought you were. In fact, I don't think I want you here at all!" I went into the garden and picked up the big bullfrog. Perhaps I squeezed the creature a little too hard for it suddenly emitted a loud roar, which caught me quite by surprise. I returned it to the river from where it had come. A few days later I discovered the same animal lurking in the vegetable garden, and there it remained for the balance of the summer. There were very few pests in the vegetable garden that year as a result of its voracious appetite. One day I discovered the bullfrog motionless under a small shrub beside the vegetable garden, looking absolutely enormous. There it remained, unmoving, for a full 24 hours. I have a strong suspicion that it did finally manage to capture and eat one of the young robins that I had recently released into the garden.

FEEDING BABY ROBINS

Over the years I received a steady supply of robins from the Centre, usually about a dozen at a time, from spring until early fall. They were wonderful birds because they were so friendly. If I were to sit on the steps leading to the lawn, the young robins would descend upon me, sitting on my head and shoulders, perching on my knees and feet. They would talk to me the whole time, chattering incessantly. I wished that I could understand 'robinese'.

I was alarmed the day that I walked around the corner of the house and found many of the young robins sprawled askew in my flowerbed. At first I thought they were ill. I consulted my reference books and learned that robins like to sunbathe: the vitamin D generated is helpful in resisting pests and parasites that inhabit their feathers. The robins were equally fond of bathing in water. By the time they had finished their vigorous splashing, it was usually necessary for me to refill the birdbath. So crowded was the birdbath at times that not all the robins could squeeze in. The less fortunate ones tended to congregate under the birdbath, where they were beneficiaries of all the water being splashed about by their peers above. Robins were a great deal of fun.

I received a call one summer day from a knowledgeable birder who appeared to have a fledgling albino robin on her lawn. I gave her the usual advice in this circumstance: before doing anything, watch the bird for at least an hour and see if an adult bird comes to feed it. In this case no adult bird appeared so I suggested that she bring it over to me. It was a most unusual bird with its white feathers, short tail, yellow beak, red eyes and pale legs — a genuine, hundred-percent albino. I kept it in the house together with other robins of the same age. The albino quickly made friends with one of the normal robins. The two chummed around and roosted together at night in my spider plant. In due course they went outside into a ground cage.

I consulted with Roy Ivor, who maintained large aviaries in southern Ontario. His experience with albino robins was not encouraging. He had once acquired a family of three albinos, which exhibited aggressive and aberrant behaviour. They attacked and killed an evening grosbeak with which they were sharing their cage. Reckoning that the albinos would not survive release because of their high visibility, Roy decided to keep them in his aviary. One albino female mated with a normal male robin. When her eggs hatched, she promptly ate the babies. That was the only information I had about raising albino robins — it was not promising.

In spite of the likelihood of a quick demise due to its conspicuous colouration, I decided to release the young albino in the usual manner. I opened its ground cage, and after a brief period, it emerged and flew up into a large willow tree. When I went out the following morning to feed the recently released robins, they descended from the surrounding trees and lined up on the picnic table to be fed. Fourteen robins were present and accounted for, but no albino. I was saddened but not surprised. My sadness proved to be short-lived, however; a few hours later I was overjoyed to see the white bird hopping about on the lawn. It did appear at the next feeding and stayed in the garden for ten days before disappearing. This was the usual pattern as there was insufficient food in my garden to support so many robins. I did receive one subsequent report of a white robin farther south along the river; that was the last news that

I received. It was as good an outcome as I could have hoped for. It was certainly a happier ending than that of another young robin that fluttered away on its maiden flight and was immediately picked off by a marauding hawk.

Kathy would often give me robins and starlings at the same time. Because these two species are fairly compatible and eat similar food, I often fed them together. In the joint feeding process, it quickly became obvious how much more intelligent were the starlings — they are smart, but nasty, birds. I am really not fond of them at all but I try not to hate them too much. I particularly recall the time that I received a large tin box stuffed with 13 baby starlings from Kathy. I started them off in cages in the house as usual. They were noisy; they smelt; and their feathers were greasy. I was not impressed with these birds at all. I soon released them outside where they joined a collection of 14 young robins. I fed these 27 birds on the hour, every hour, throughout the day on a picnic table.

The robins were used to coming when I called them, and the starlings immediately caught on to this routine. The mix of young birds lined up on the picnic table, practically covering its entire surface. I went around the table with a feeding stick, delivering a morsel to each gaping, screeching mouth, and then prepared to do a second round. By the end of the first circuit, the starlings had learned that if they scooted over to the beginning of the line, they would be fed much more quickly than if they waited where they were. The queue-jumping starlings jostled aside the bewildered robins, which became very bad-tempered in the process. The robins never did figure out what the quick-witted starlings were up to.

Gradually different fledgling bird species began coming to me from a variety of sources. One day a friend called with an unusual request. She had been caring for two green heron fledglings, and they required an appropriate locale for release. I knew of a marsh that was inhabited by green herons and reckoned that it might be the best location since the habitat was clearly suitable. We decided that I should look after these birds for a few days pending release. I set up a child's wading pool in the yard and placed a wooden box adjacent to it. The herons liked their box very much: they got on top of it and sat. Curiously, they didn't crouch or squat with their legs underneath them like most birds. They preferred to sit on their rumps with their long legs sticking out in front of them, looking like sunbathers. It was a most comical sight! After a few days we loaded up the green herons and took them to the marsh, where we released them and left, hoping for the best. Once released the herons would never return, so there was no way that we could continue feeding them like their parents would have in the wild. We could only hope that the herons would quickly learn to feed themselves.

GREEN HERON
PHOTO BY JUDITH GUSTAFSSON

Though I kept robins in cages, I never did so with swallows. I strung perching wires around the sun porch for these free-flying birds. Over the years I raised three species of the Swallow family — tree swallows, barn swallows and purple martins. I was astonished by the difference in intelligence between the barn swallows and the tree swallows. The barn swallows were vastly superior to the feeble-minded tree swallows. When I got up each morning to begin the feeding rounds, one of the tree swallows would inevitably have gone missing in the house. I would usually find the errant bird down on the floor in some corner or lurking underneath a piece of furniture. One morning I was particularly baffled in my search for a missing tree swallow. I looked in room after room before finally discovering the miscreant sitting in the coils of the boxspring underneath my bed.

Purple martins are the largest of the swallows and fiendishly difficult to feed. These uncooperative martins require live food, such as mealworms, and sometimes it was necessary to force-feed them. I never had very many martins, and for that I was grateful. It was always difficult to give them enough food. It was these martins that caused me to earn one of three speeding tickets that I acquired during my driving career. When I looked into my bucket of mealworms one morning, I discovered to my dismay that none were left. This necessitated a quick trip to Kathy's home to replenish my supply. On the way I passed an oncoming police car, and glancing in the rear view mirror, I observed it making a U-turn — surely not after me? Alas, yes, the red lights came on, and I dutifully stopped. A young officer approached my car.

"How fast do you think you were going when you overtook that car?" he demanded to know.

"Oh, how fast was I going?" I countered innocently.

· ·

"Too fast!" came his reply. "Enough for a fine and three demerit points."

"What?" I cried. "How often do you think baby purple martins need to be fed? Every half hour on mealworms, and I have run out. So I am rushing to get more before they starve to death."

The poor constable! Of all the excuses that he had heard previously, I am quite sure that he had never heard one like this. Fortunately for me, the kindly officer reduced the fine, thereby eliminating the demerit points. I thanked him profusely and drove away very much relieved. He and his colleagues probably had a good laugh over the idiosyncrasies of white-haired lady birders.

One year I received a baby eastern kingbird, which proved to be a most delightful bird. After release it liked to sit in the top of the large willow tree. When it was feeding time, I would go outside and call. The kingbird would fly down and take mealworms from my hand. A young man came to visit me while the kingbird was still in my garden. "Would you like to feed a kingbird?" I inquired. "Hold out your hand with this mealworm." Moments later the kingbird swooped down onto his outstretched hand as a look of rapture swept across his face.

I once received a family of four baby blue jays; I had an interesting time with them. Shortly after I released them, a noisy thunderstorm dumped an enormous deluge of rain. The jays became completely waterlogged on the ground and were unable to fly. I decided that it would be best if they came back into the house to dry off. I quickly collected three of them but could not find the fourth. I searched and searched, and finally found the little devil hiding amongst a patch of ferns. I collected the drenched bird and reunited it with its siblings.

After the jays had dried off, I released them for a second time. Like most birds, baby jays call to their parents to indicate their location when they want to be fed. One of the jay fledglings flew up to the roof of the house and began to call loudly, attracting the attention of the resident robins. Robins cannot abide blue jays in nesting season because jays will devour both their eggs and their nestlings. A mob of robins hastily assembled to attack the intruder, doing so with such vigour that they bowled the young jay off the roof and down into the hedge from where I rescued it yet again.

Jay fledglings are very demanding youngsters — they require feeding by their parents for up to two months after leaving the nest. For this reason jays never have more than one brood per season. My four fledglings would line up on the fence surrounding the dog compound and shriek for food. Three of the four would eagerly eat mealworms from a saucer, but the fourth would merely sit, open its mouth and expect to be hand-fed. The weaning process, which continued for five weeks, was ultimately successful. Despite their various misadventures along the way, all four progressed to maturity and gradually drifted away.

One summer I received two orphaned juvenile common nighthawks. They were enchanting – and strange! They passed their daylight hours in the living room, where they would spend the entire day asleep on the back of an armchair. When dusk approached, they would awaken, stand up and stretch their wings right over their heads with a wonderfully fluid motion. Then they would shake themselves and get composed. When the wake-up ritual was complete, they would take off, flying gracefully and silently around the house, like a pair of great mottled moths. They were very difficult birds to handle because they refused to gape to be fed. I don't know how their parents would have fed them. They have a very tiny bill that opens into a great cavernous mouth. It was necessary for me to force-feed them, which meant prying open their little beaks with a tooth-pick, a technique that I had perfected over the years.

When the time came for release, I gave some thought as to where to do so. There did not appear to be any nighthawks in my vicinity for I had never heard any of their characteristic peeping calls high overhead. They were far more common closer to the city where their calls could be heard all night. Friends from Ottawa kindly offered to take the young pair there and release them where nighthawks were known to hunt. It was the best that we could do under the circumstances. We hoped that they would hear their own kind and join them. We had no way of knowing whether our scheme would work, but at least we would give them an opportunity to succeed. With any luck the ample nourishment available in the insect-laden sky would be enough to sustain them.

I once received a beautifully woven nest containing a complete family of baby Baltimore orioles. Usually an oriole nest is very strong and does not come adrift from its branch. One can often see them still hanging in trees during winter — they rarely blow down. Perhaps this particular nest had been woven by a novice weaver for it had given way and fallen intact; it contained four young birds on the verge of flying. Rather than remove them from the nest, I decided that it would be easier to leave them inside. I secured the nest to my little crabapple tree and fed the nestlings at their nest hole just as their parents would have done: only the menu changed. These elegant orioles were gentle, friendly birds with a unique, silky plumage; eventually they emerged from their nest, foraged in the crabapple tree for a few days, and then departed.

Four young American goldfinches were delivered to me on another occasion. They were pale imitations of their colourful parents and proved to be the most demanding of babies. They shrieked constantly with a single, high-pitched note that was quite troublesome. They were always hungry, had very small mouths, and like the nighthawks, had to be fed with a toothpick. I fed them the standard food mix that I used for most of the baby birds. For insect-eating birds I would mix in some of the dried insect mix that one can buy for caged birds. Kathy had some wonderfully complex food mixes for all her birds. I would add some vitamins to my mixes but always wondered about the adequacy of the food and whether some essential ingredient might be missing. In any case the food mix seemed to work perfectly well for these young goldfinches; they continued to develop and make a cacophonous racket in the garden.

It was while I had the goldfinches that a telephone repairman came to the house to fix a problem with my line. As he was leaving, I looked out my window to see him walking across the yard with his arm raised: on it sat all four goldfinches, no doubt hoping for a handout. A look of wonderment crossed his face as he walked. I am sure it was an experience that he will never forget.

Not all my bird-raising attempts went as planned, but my sparrow-feeding experiment was quite successful. Surprisingly, common house sparrows were especially problematic. While in the nest they ate regularly and behaved normally. Once released, they seemed to prefer suicide — they would refuse to eat. On one occasion when I was being frustrated by a young house sparrow, I remembered that I had house sparrows occupying one of my nestboxes. It was after one of those epic battles that the tree swallows had lost. I was curious to see how the adult nesting pair would respond if I put the young bird into their nestbox. With any luck they would feed it because parental bird instinct to feed is so very strong. I climbed the ladder, looked into the box and saw a clutch of eggs. Then I stuffed the young sparrow into the box and stepped away to see what would happen.

When one of the parents returned to resume sitting on the eggs, it paused at the entrance to look inside. One wonders what its little brain processed when it saw a fully developed fledgling inside its nest! Shortly thereafter the second parent arrived and joined its mate hanging at the entrance. The sight of the adult birds triggered squawking from the fledgling, and not long after I saw one of the parents returning to the box with food for its uninvited guest. This story had a happy ending: the little fledgling survived, and the rest of the brood hatched despite the presence of the noisy intruder.

FOOD MIXES FOR FLEDGLING BIRDS

I often received phone calls from people with very small baby birds, or birds without feathers, so that it was impossible to identify the species. The emergency food for these birds is lightly cooked scrambled eggs. If you have baby Pablum on hand, you can add a little to the eggs. Then feed to the baby birds with a toothpick. Give the birds a little water, but not too much in case you drown them. It is possible, depending on the circumstances, that an abandoned baby may have become dehydrated. Once again use a toothpick to give the birds tiny droplets of water. An alternative to scrambled eggs is canned dog meat, preferably beef-based. It is also acceptable to mix a little dog meat into the scrambled egg mixture. When you have fed and watered the young birds, contact your nearest Wildlife Rescue Centre for further advice.

Chapter 7:
RATTLES THE KINGFISHER

....

In all the years that I was helping to care for and release fledgling birds, I think that my most favourite memory is of a young belted kingfisher that I named Rattles. Belted kingfishers are unusual in that the females are more colourful than the males. While both sexes sport blue bands across their white breasts, the females also display an attractive chestnut band. Kingfishers were a common sight from our property beside the Rideau River. Flying low to the water with powerful wing strokes, these chunky blue-grey birds with ragged crests would fly up and down the river with great regularity. Their flight was often punctuated by the loud, piercing rattle that is characteristic of this species.

Kingfishers would seek out favourite perches, like the branches of trees overhanging the river. From one of these excellent vantage points they would sit patiently, scanning the water below for the minnows that form the major part of their diet. If the perching technique proved unsuccessful, they would try a different approach — hovering in one location over the river for a few seconds, and then moving on to another. When a minnow was spotted, the kingfisher would dive in pursuit, crashing into the water with a terrific splash. In most cases the bird would emerge with a wriggling morsel of silver in its sturdy bill, but of course not every dive was successful.

A MALE BELTED KINGFISHER
PHOTO BY TONY BECK

Kingfishers do not build nests like most other birds. Rather, a pair excavates a nesting hole in a bank of soft earth or sand. Such a hole may be located, for example, in a riverbank, a highway cut or a sandpit. A tunnel, usually one or two metres long, leads to an enlarged chamber where the female will lay her eggs. This tunnel slopes gently up to the chamber in order to prevent the accumulation of water inside. In the year that Rattles came to me, rapid transit construction underway within Ottawa required the excavation of sandy banks along both sides of the route. Unfortunately, a pair of kingfishers had chosen to do a prior excavation, making their nesting hole in one of the banks.

My birding friend Ray Holland was aware of the kingfisher nest and had been watching the comings and goings of the adult pair as they fed their offspring. To his alarm he realized that the construction crew was coming within striking distance of the nest hole. The crew had begun to place siding along the unstable sandy banks, an act that would cover up the entrance to the nest hole. While it appeared that some of the fledglings had flown away, a distinct rattling sound from within the nest hole indicated that at least one youngster was still present. Ray decided to approach the construction foreman and explained the problem. The foreman was sympathetic and offered Ray a shovel so that he could dig into the bank and rescue any baby birds. So Ray began to dig, and dig, and dig. He found that the tunnel wound deep into the bank, up and over a buried electrical cable. In the enlarged nesting cavity at the very end cowered a single, young kingfisher. Poor Ray! He had wriggled all the way into this hole to rescue a kingfisher, and now he was faced with the challenge of squirming backwards out of the hole while carrying his precious cargo. I thought he deserved a medal for his heroic actions.

So it was that Ray brought Rattles to me. We found a small wooden box with a door, covered its floor with sand to simulate the original nest, and placed the little bird inside. Then we went to the local bait shop to see if we could arrange for a supply of minnows. They were happy to provide minnows, both live and recently deceased, free of charge. I began feeding the dead minnows to Rattles, reckoning that they would be equivalent to what he had been receiving from his parents. When it was time to feed him, I would approach the wooden box and scratch its exterior. Rattles quickly associated that sound with feeding time and would respond with a loud and enthusiastic rattle, hence his nickname.

Human mothers are advised to monitor excreta from their offspring to ensure that their digestive systems are working properly and to maintain a sanitary environment. As a surrogate kingfisher mother, I did likewise. To my consternation this bird didn't seem to be excreting at all. Food was going in, but nothing was coming out — it was most peculiar. I began to worry whether there was an intestinal blockage or some dietary deficiency. When I read up on kingfishers to learn more about their needs and habits, I discovered that young kingfishers do not produce any solid waste at all. Their stomach acidity is so strong that fish bones are completely dissolved. As a result, urine and bowel wastes are combined into a single liquid, which the nestlings deposit at the rear of their nest cavity. Sure enough when I looked closely into the back of the box, there was a wet patch in one of the bottom corners. So all was well — and that was a great relief! Curiously, the ability of young kingfishers to completely consume fish bones and scales disappears as they grow into adulthood. When they are mature, kingfishers disgorge pellets of fish bones, scales and other indigestible material.

Feathers are vitally important for birds: they are essential for insulation, camouflage, mating displays and flight. Feathers keep birds warm in cold weather and cool in hot weather. They are crucial for incubating a clutch of eggs or sheltering a brood of youngsters. Feathers provide camouflage for many species — ground-feeding birds like sparrows are often a brownish colour, while most kingfishers are a bluish colour, which is difficult for aquatic prey to see against the sky. The condition and brightness of feathers is a good general indicator of a bird's health, and as such, influence potential mating partners. Feathers consist of a shaft and branching vanes, which contain barbs and barbules that interlock to provide the lift necessary for flight. Most baby birds develop feathers gradually in a rather patchy manner in different places at different times. Not so belted kingfishers — on the fourteenth day of their development, their offspring 'bloom'. On the eve of the fourteenth day, Rattles bristled with unopened feather shafts, like the quills of a baby hedgehog. By morning the vanes on these shafts had all unfolded into feathers. Rattles went to bed a hedgehog and awoke a kingfisher. It was absolutely magical!

In the wild, adult kingfishers teach their offspring how to dive and catch fish. Adults will take their young to a secluded spot to first catch and then stun a minnow. The minnow is then dropped back into the water where it will remain floating on the surface, making an easy catch for a novice kingfisher. In such a way young kingfishers gain experience and are ultimately able to catch live minnows on their own.

How on earth could we simulate that sort of training? As stand-in kingfisher parents, Ray and I pondered our options for teaching Rattles how to catch his own food. We first set up perches around the children's wading pool and placed live minnows in it. Then we brought out Rattles from his box and placed him on the perch where he could see the minnows.

The young bird was clearly very interested in the minnows, but that was as far as it went. Any idea of diving in and catching one did not seem to occur to him. He continued to eat just from his nestbox where I fed him by hand. We tried again the following afternoon, but to our dismay, he flew away soon after we placed him on his perch. He disappeared into the neighbour's garden but returned later in the day to land on one of the bird feeders hanging in the willow tree. I approached him cautiously and offered a minnow but he refused to take it. With the passage of time I became more anxious: as far as I was aware, Rattles had been out of his cage and without food for nearly five days. I mulled over the problem again and thought back to the time that I had raised a couple of gulls. I had placed some dead fish in the birdbath where the gulls had swiftly devoured them. What if I tried the same technique with Rattles? I put a few live minnows in the birdbath and went inside the house to observe what would happen. Several hours later, to my great joy, Rattles landed on the edge of the birdbath, and after some hesitation, stabbed into the water and caught several minnows. I was elated. Ray and I thought that we were away.

The following morning I arose and went outside to survey the situation. There I discovered evidence of what appeared to be a tragedy — blue kingfisher feathers lay scattered under the birdbath. I had once witnessed a neighbouring cat catch an adult robin from the birdbath, and so I feared the worst. Ray and I were distraught and went into mourning over the presumed demise of our young bird. Several weeks later a curious incident occurred at the wharf of my next-door neighbours, who were readying their motor launch for a boat trip. A number of people were already milling about on deck when a kingfisher landed on the railing at the stern of the vessel. It sat there very close to the passengers, quite unconcerned by their presence. Kingfishers are ordinarily extremely shy birds so this was most unusual behaviour. I felt certain that it must have been Rattles, but of course I had no way of knowing. Not only did the kingfisher remain on the railing while the boat was being loaded, but when the boaters set out, it went with them! Ray came to visit me the following year during the spring migration. We were standing on the lawn when a kingfisher flew down the river from the south. It sailed directly over the house and rattled loudly as it passed. Ray was quite sure that this was Rattles returning. At least we like to think that it was.

Chapter 8:
JOEY THE PIGEON

· ·

Joey, the seafaring pigeon, came sailing down the river on a small ice floe on Easter Sunday in 1974. The Rideau River had recently broken up, and I was raking up winter debris along the riverbank. As the floe came nearer, my attention was attracted to a small, dumpy figure. It appeared to be a tailless bird unable to fly. A rescue attempt was obviously required. The current swept the ice floe tantalizingly close to shore but just beyond the reach of my fan rake. To my amazement the little bird, perhaps sensing that this was his last chance for rescue, launched himself into the frigid waters. He swam toward me doing a creditable imitation of the butterfly stroke. "Come on!" I cried, fearing that the icy water was sapping his strength, "You can do it!" After a few tense moments he came within reach of my fan rake; I slipped it underneath him and lifted him out of the water.

I rushed the sopping wet bird into the house, wrapped him in a towel and placed him in a carton. Then I placed the carton on a heat register to help him recover from his chilly plunge. When I returned an hour later, I found the young bird sitting up and preening, apparently unscathed by his misadventures. I looked at his emerging plumage and realized that he was a rock dove (also known as the common pigeon), partially fledged and with a minute tail barely two centimetres long. His grey and black plumage was ornamented with what resembled strands of yellow thread. These strands were thicker around his head, like a tattered halo, giving him a rather raffish look. The pigeon was clearly unable to fly. I imagine that he must have fallen from an upstream bridge and fortuitously landed on an ice floe. The nearest such bridge was eight kilometres upstream so he had endured a long, cold journey before washing up on my doorstep. I decided to name him Joey.

I pondered what to do about food for my new charge. I had little experience in the care and feeding of fledgling birds at this time. I consulted reference books and learned how fledgling pigeons eat: they reach into their mother's crop for pre-digested food. Unlike a songbird Joey did not open his beak when he was hungry: this made feeding him rather difficult. I located an eyedropper, prepared a thin gruel of oatmeal and hard-boiled egg, and then pumped a small amount into him. The first attempt was only partially successful. The young pigeon clearly did not enjoy the process or the food, some of which spilled onto his chest feathers. There it became sticky and bothered him. (Later, I learned that had I placed the food mixture in a small pill bottle that resembled his mother's crop, he would have fed himself more naturally.) Nonetheless we carried on, and this rudimentary food mix sustained him for several days, during which time Joey made two decisions: that I was his mother; and that corn niblets were specially designed for little pigeons. Although he delighted in gorging on these niblets, I thought he should have a varied diet and so included other grains, softened at first and then dry. One day Joey practiced flapping his developing wings while standing in the middle of his feeding dish, scattering seeds in all directions.

As a youngster Joey possessed outsized pink feet, which he had some difficulty controlling. He would lift them very high with each step and gradually developed the motor skills to make them more manageable. He became adept at taking three flying hops to propel himself up to the back of the armchair, where he could sit in the sun, preen and peer outside. At first he slept in a carton and went to bed at precisely half past five. He would get restless and cranky, letting me know that it was time for bed. As he matured, he began to stay up later, and one night he refused to settle down at all. In due course I allowed him out of his carton and watched with amusement at his attempts to find an acceptable roosting place. The lampshade, which swayed dangerously, was clearly unsuitable, while the curtain rail was too narrow. Finally with a little persuasion, he settled on the top of a door, which became one of his special places.

Joey liked to sit on my knee, nibble my finger and peep inquiringly. When I said goodnight to him, he would answer with two sleepy peeps from his door. He slept squatting on his feet with his beak nestled in the puffed-up feathers of his chest. Eventually his flying strength and agility improved to the point where I felt that he could be taken outside. At first Joey was quite nervous and kept close to the house, where he would look for places to hide. He spent long periods of time in the doghouse, sleeping in the straw. Little by little he became more accustomed to the outdoors and became braver; he even began to fly outside voluntarily. Thereafter I let him come and go at will through an open window. Joey was now fully feathered with pink and iridescent green feathers on his neck. One day a strange rumbling heralded the beginning of a coo, which was quickly followed by his strutting routine. He would walk in tight circles with his neck feathers puffed out, cooing loudly. He would also welcome his 'family' home with this routine.

The first night that Joey slept outside, he roosted on the windowsill near my bedroom window but later chose the top of a birdhouse. The family of tree swallows occupying this nestbox did not take kindly to their 'roof guest'. With swoops and dives they attempted to dislodge him from his perch, but Joey proved a stubborn and fearless bird. For a short period of time, the swallows ceased their attack and focussed on feeding their offspring. But when their young were ready to fly, the swallows resumed their attack so savagely that Joey abandoned that side of the house entirely.

Inside the house Joey was becoming very attached to his 'family', which included our large dog, Skipper. Not surprisingly given his upbringing, Joey seemed unsure of his identity at times. His strutting display was most often performed in front of Skipper (or anyone else's dog for that matter). Remarkably, he escaped harm despite his reckless tameness. He developed a tendency to fly down and land on a human head or shoulder. As he was prone to peck, this made for an unnerving and occasionally painful experience. On the positive side it was always a delight to be awoken by the patter of his little feet and gentle cooing. Joey delighted in finding a recumbent human form upon which he could march up and down, billing and cooing. Eventually he would settle down in a hollow and make soft, growly noises to himself. Sometimes he would cuddle up to a pair of shoes, but if anyone approached he would jump to his feet and begin cooing.

Joey had a particular interest in supervising all my gardening activities. He would stay close to me, looking for tidbits and occasionally landing on my bent back. Once I nearly buried him in a large hole that he decided to inspect just as I was lowering a plant into it. A fine spray from the garden hose would send him into ecstasy. He would roll over on one side and then the other, lifting his wings and letting the water play over his 'armpits'. His feathers were so thick and waterproof that he had to fluff them up in order for the water to reach his skin. Joey loved to bathe even in the coldest weather. A mere trickle of water dripping from the roof would be sufficient to induce him to shower.

Joey preferred to be indoors and would seize any opportunity to come inside. This led to an assortment of accidents that might well have killed a less resilient bird. The first accident occurred when he was caught by a closing screen door and left flapping wildly, suspended by his head. I was nearby and rushed to release him. Although he fell to the floor, he quickly recovered with no lasting damage. In the second accident he became caught by a leg. His struggles to free himself left him lame for several weeks, but he eventually recovered. The third accident was the most perilous. Joey had just flown out the window when he made an unexpected U-turn and flew back just as I was lowering the window. It caught him across the shoulders and pinned him hard. It was a miracle that he survived at all. This incident damaged his cooing mechanism for a period of time: he was very quiet for a day or two but ultimately regained his voice.

I thought that it would be a good idea to acquire a female pigeon in order to give Joey company and help him through his identity crisis. I obtained a juvenile pigeon and named her Josie. On her first night Josie took over Joey's sleeping quarters on the door, thereby banishing him outside to the top of the now-empty birdhouse. The two pigeons were together all winter and into spring, when Josie developed breeding plumage for the first time. To my dismay Josie turned out to be male! The duly re-christened José was quicker off the mark than poor Joey. He swiftly found a female and left home, leaving Joey alone once more. Joey became ever more dependent upon us, and I despaired that he would ever realize his true identity.

As is often the case, love proved to be the solution to the problem. Joey encountered a charming little female, and little by little she won him over. The two birds continued to visit daily for food but never stayed long. Their visits became less frequent, and I thought that perhaps they had joined a flock of pigeons across the river. Hunting season began, adding a new concern, so I rejoiced greatly when the pair re-appeared one afternoon. Joey was even sporting a smart new set of feathers. He was wilder now and had evidently achieved what I had always hoped for him — a free life in the wild with his own kind. Joey's indomitable spirit and insatiable curiosity made his stay a memorable one. I trust that he lived free in sturdy independence for many years thereafter.

Chapter 9:
WRITING FOR THE OTTAWA *CITIZEN*

....

Wilf Bell was the bird columnist for the Ottawa *Citizen* in the early 1970s. Although I had never met him, I was a steady contributor of bird sightings. As a result of these reports we were in regular communication, which often resulted in long telephone conversations. In one of these chats Wilf advised me that he would be returning to England, and to my considerable surprise inquired whether I would like to take over the birding column. I replied that I would think about it and let him know. I mulled over the offer and thought, "I think I'm now sufficiently conversant with Canadian birds to do it. And I know that I can string a sentence together reasonably well." That settled it!

My first column appeared in print in 1974. It was March, a time of the year when migrants return. I decided to write about the blackish birds that tended to arrive simultaneously — red-winged blackbirds, common grackles, brown-headed cowbirds, European starlings and the like — and described the key identifying marks by which one could distinguish them. Wilf and I finally met in person after I had drafted this inaugural column. I gratefully accepted his splendid offer to critique my writing before I submitted it to the *Citizen*. Wilf arrived at my home with several of his children in tow. After exchanging pleasantries I handed him the proof and nervously awaited his assessment. I could feel the tension in the room as he scanned the document with his brow furrowing. When he had finished reading, he looked up and asked, "Do you realize that I didn't have the faintest idea whether you could actually write a column or not?" He then added that it was better than he had expected; in fact, he was rather pleased with it. And so began the first of my 39 years as the birding columnist for the Ottawa *Citizen*. In those early days the general rule of thumb was that I would write two handwritten pages of draft text and then type it. This would provide an approximately suitable word count for the newspaper.

Two of my earliest and most faithful contributors were teenagers Bruce Di Labio and Mark Gawn, who spent most of their waking hours riding their bicycles along the Ottawa River searching out interesting birds. John Kelly was another young man with a love of birds and the artistic skill to illustrate them. In the early years he regularly contributed artwork appropriate to the content of that week's column. Although John's art was rendered in colour, it was reproduced in black and white because newspapers were not printing in colour in those early years. Initially the focus of my column was very much on bird sightings in the immediate Ottawa area. These reports were always communicated to me by telephone. With the advent of computers and email communication, the reporting of bird sightings expanded greatly throughout eastern Ontario — to Montreal in the east, Wakefield in the north, Algonquin Park in the west, and to the Saint Lawrence Seaway in the south.

When digital photography burst onto the scene, many keen birders adopted the new technology with enthusiasm. Sighting reports arriving by email were often accompanied by the most beautiful colour photographs, which greatly enhanced the appearance of the column. Most weeks I would receive about 50 sighting reports, many with photographs. This number increased so much during migration times that with all the material I received, I could have written three columns each week.

It was challenging to choose amongst the various photo submissions, especially when I received multiple images of the same bird. It was actually my *Citizen* editor who made the final selections from the group of photos that I would submit, a fact that I had to explain repeatedly to contributors disappointed at not seeing their photo in the paper. When the raptor populations began to rebound after DDT was banned, I was inundated with pictures of immature hawks and asked to identify them. Even the identification of adult hawks, with their different colour phases and variable plumage, has always been difficult for me. Juvenile hawks, with their lack of prominent marking, are even more challenging. Fortunately, I had the assistance of a reliable raptor expert, Tony Beck, to whom I could forward these requests.

Many of the calls that I received were not sighting reports but rather requests for assistance in identifying an unfamiliar bird that did not appear to be in field guides.

"I can't find it in my book!" was the great cry of anguish from such a caller.

It was very difficult helping these birders. I quickly discovered that most people were very poor at identifying the size of a bird. It didn't seem to dawn on them that a bird seen up close would appear much larger than one sitting atop a fifteen-metre pine tree. To initiate an attempt at identification, I would ask simply, "Was it the size of a sparrow, a robin or a crow?" This question usually elicited a hesitant response after a period of reflection. Powers of observation varied wildly from one caller to the next. Callers would assert that they had identified an unusual species at their feeders. It often transpired that a bird so identified could only be found in the Arctic or the Pacific or some other distant locale. Too often I learned that the callers had not consulted the range maps to see if their purported sighting could be expected in eastern Ontario. I recall a conversation that I once had with ornithologist Dr. Earl Godfrey, the renowned author of *Birds of Canada*. He told me of a call that he had received from an excited birder who described an unfamiliar bird with such hyperbole that Dr. Godfrey thought that he should investigate what sounded like a stray tropical species. Imagine his surprise when he arrived to find a common northern flicker!

One cold winter day I received a telephone call from an excited observer reporting four 'baby grosbeaks' at her feeder. Of course they were simply overwintering American goldfinches, which have yellow, black and white colouration similar to that of evening grosbeaks. I found it disappointing that some people were so unaware of the normal cycles of nature. In this case it never occurred to the caller that with very few exceptions, birds do not nest and rear offspring in the middle of winter.

The most memorable report that I received in my 39 years as bird columnist came one winter day from an Ottawa lady who was certain that she had a penguin in her pine tree. I was speechless! I hardly knew where to begin. I advised her that penguins are strictly a Southern Hemisphere species. I reminded her that penguins do not fly, nor do they perch in trees. Eventually I was able to disabuse the caller of her misidentification. That was certainly the strangest of the various odd reports that I received over the years.

Whenever a rare bird was in the news, copycat sightings became a common phenomenon. If such a sighting were reported in my column, almost inevitably I would receive a call from someone during the following week saying, "I've got one of those at my feeder." It was after the exciting news of the possible sighting of an ivory-billed woodpecker in Arkansas that I received a call from a local farmer who assured me categorically that he had one in his field. No amount of persuasion could convince the man that this was highly unlikely. Ivory-billed woodpeckers are probably extinct (there have not been any confirmed sightings for decades); they do not migrate; and they prefer inundated forests, like those of coastal bayous. It is hardly a species to be found grubbing in a farmer's open field. Most likely it was a pileated woodpecker, some of which have very pale beaks. Despite my dubious assessment that man will go to his grave convinced that he had seen an ivory-billed woodpecker in his field.

In spite of my misgivings and even occasional frustration with birders who did not consult the range maps in their field guides, I must acknowledge that on rare occasions some highly unusual birds did in fact find their way into the Ottawa region. Two very unexpected sightings during my career attracted much media attention — a Chilean flamingo and a yellow-nosed albatross. In cases like these, the Rare Bird Committee of the Ottawa Field-Naturalists' Club would confirm the accuracy of the identification. Digital photography proved an asset in this task too. With their powerful lenses birding photographers were often able to get excellent close-up photographs, which could either confirm or refute an identification.

In the early years of the column, one of the most distressing issues that I had to deal with on a regular basis was what to tell people who called about orphaned or injured birds. There was simply no help available at that time. Most veterinarians have no training or experience in dealing with wild birds. In the Ottawa area there was one veterinarian who might be persuaded to look at a bird, but certainly not if it were a pigeon, starling or crow. When Kathy Nihei established the Wild Bird Care Centre in 1981, I rejoiced that there would be a facility for injured and orphaned birds about which I could inform my readers.

Halfway through my writing career, the Ottawa *Citizen* advised me that I must submit my column in electronic format, which would eliminate the need for a staffer to re-enter my typewritten column. Until this time I had always delivered my column in person, either directly to my editor or to the *Citizen*'s newsroom. In 1994 at the age of 80, I purchased my first (expensive) computer and reluctantly entered the digital age. It was not entirely a happy experience! I engaged the services of a tutor, a young Irishman, and with his assistance managed to email my first electronic column to the *Citizen*. I kept a little black book of computer commands, helpful suggestions and basic troubleshooting methods. Initially I was a bit of a duffer at the computer, baffled by mysterious events that seemed to crop up at random. Once I had just completed my column when *whoosh* — it evaporated, leaving me with a blank screen. It was very upsetting! Some weeks I would receive a call from my editor:

"We have received your email with the column, but the document was blank. Would you mind re-sending?"

Other weeks the message would be:

"We have received your email, but the attachment was missing."

Oh dear!

After I moved from my home to the Orchard View Living Centre, I was frequently bailed out of assorted computer disasters thanks to the adept assistance of the younger staff members. I was also rescued regularly by Harvey Hope, my long-time computer guru, who maintained my computer via remote connection. It was Harvey who resolved problems with my email account or with my Internet service provider. To this day I maintain a love-hate relationship with my computer. It is wonderful when it works, but most frustrating when it does not.

Over the course of my long career with the *Citizen*, I interacted with a number of editors who reviewed my column. In general the editorial process went quite smoothly except on one unfortunate occasion when inattentive editing accidentally introduced the mythical 'great horned heron' to the newspaper's reading public. I was mortified when I saw the glaring mistake in print. I imagined that birders would think me a hopeless incompetent, even though the blunder was not my responsibility. With the passage of time, I am able to look back now and see the humourous side of this incident.

In March of 2013, at the beginning of my fortieth year of writing the bird column, I reached the difficult decision that it was time to retire. My advancing age, three months before my ninety-ninth birthday, had caught up to me, and the column had begun to overwhelm me. When I announced the decision in my column, I was stunned by the response from my kindly readers. Some expressed dismay:

"It's the only reason that we buy the Saturday paper," said one caller.

"We always turn to your column first," said another.

Then emails began flooding in, many from regular contributors who had been reporting sightings for years. To my surprise they thanked me again and again for the column, commenting how it had opened their eyes to nature and changed their attitudes toward the environment. In my last column I was able to thank my faithful readers:

"If it hadn't been for you, and all your reports, and all your wonderful photographs, there would not have been a column," I wrote.

The final column was accompanied by a most magnificent spread in the Ottawa *Citizen*. In the following week I continued to receive emails, cards, presents and flower arrangements. It was absolutely amazing and so very heartwarming. Internal readership surveys by the *Citizen* showed that the bird column was always one of the most-read weekend features, a fact that I found very gratifying as I retired.

Occasionally when I was away on vacation, Bruce Di Labio or Ray Holland would kindly substitute for me and write the column. Bruce had remained a faithful contributor over the years and had developed into one of Ottawa's most accomplished birders, leading birding tours across Canada and around the globe. When I retired, the *Citizen* offered the birding column to Bruce. It is a great pleasure for me to know that the column will continue in such excellent hands.

Chapter 10:
ELISHA THE FLAMINGO

. . . .

Over the years a number of very unusual birds have found their way into the Ottawa area. Some were blown off course by storms, while others were perhaps genetically defective with respect to their navigational systems. These exotic arrivals included a northern gannet (normally found along North Atlantic coastlines); a yellow-nosed albatross (native to the Indian Ocean); a purple gallinule (native to the coastline of the Caribbean Sea); and a Chilean flamingo (native to temperate regions of Ecuador, Peru, Bolivia, Chile and Argentina).

Since the Wild Bird Care Centre opened, it has rescued many birds, both injured and orphaned, as well as some rare strays. In November of 1997, birders wandering along a bank of the Ottawa River discovered one of the most unusual strays — a Chilean flamingo! Six species of these iconic pink birds exist around the world, mostly in Africa and South America. The Chilean flamingo stands more than a metre tall, and like all flamingos, is a filter feeder. Flamingos have specialized beaks that allow them to filter plankton, algae and brine shrimp from their preferred habitat — coastal mudflats, river estuaries and brine lakes. It is the beta-carotene consumed in its diet that gives the flamingo its spectacular pink colouration.

You can imagine the excitement when one of these striking birds unexpectedly appeared in the Ottawa River. With winter rapidly approaching and the certainty that the river would freeze over, Kathy Nihei decided that every effort should be made to capture and save this bird. By conducting a thorough search on the Internet, she discovered that the flamingo, dubbed Elisha, was not wild but rather an escapee from a bird refuge in Litchfield, Connecticut. Elisha was a free-flying bird, and for whatever reason, had abandoned her mate in Litchfield and wandered north. Elisha was in good condition when she was discovered; initially it appeared that she was finding sufficient food in the soft margins of the river to sustain herself. She was certainly alert enough to evade the first few attempts to capture her. Over the course of a month, the weather gradually cooled off, and the first frost settled onto the ground. During this time the unfolding saga of Elisha and her activities became a significant news story. The Ottawa *Citizen* took a particular interest in the tale of the flamingo and issued bulletins almost daily.

On several occasions Elisha had been observed feeding where a small creek widened into a shallow pool before emptying into the Ottawa River. Kathy decided to set a net trap nearby, but it was to no avail. Elisha's condition weakened noticeably over the course of the next month. One night the temperature dipped so low that ice formed in the shallows of the pool, and Elisha found her legs frozen in. She struggled successfully to free herself the following morning, but the effort tired her. Later that day Steve Macklin, one of the volunteers from the Wild Bird Care Centre, was able to approach her and throw a net over her. Steve clasped Elisha in his arms, wrapped her in a blanket, and brought her back to the Centre.

In such circumstances wild birds frequently become very stressed, but Elisha was familiar with human contact because of her life at the Connecticut bird refuge. She was quite comfortable when placed in a bathtub of lukewarm water, the first stop for any waterfowl brought to the Centre. At one point she began to scratch energetically at the bottom of the tub before switching her attention to a feeding dish of 'flamingo kibble'. She was clearly very hungry, which was not surprising considering the scarcity of suitable food in the Ottawa River. Within a week Elisha regained her normal weight, and her strength returned.

Kathy was able to organize the return of Elisha to her refuge in Connecticut with the kind assistance of Air Canada, which has been very generous over the years in providing homeward flights for stray birds. The *Citizen* newspaper concluded its coverage of Elisha by sending a reporter along on the flight. Elisha seemed to be quite content to be reunited with her mate and flock after her vacation adventure. I was very pleased that this story of a wayward bird had a happy ending.

Chapter 11:
JACKO THE PARROT

....

Jacko, an African grey parrot, was born into captivity in a pet shop from where he was purchased by a young couple who thought they would enjoy owning a parrot. Unfortunately, these owners did not understand the emotional and societal requirements of parrots. They went to work and left Jacko alone for large portions of the day. Parrots are highly social birds, and Jacko suffered from his enforced isolation. His owners were sufficiently observant to realize that the parrot was extremely unhappy. He was on the verge of pulling out his feathers and biting his feet, actions that indicated a highly stressed bird. They wisely decided to pass Jacko on to the MacIntyres, a family who lived on a nearby farm. Just two years later Mrs. MacIntyre passed away unexpectedly, and Jacko, then aged four, came to live with me. He was quite unhappy in the first few days and refused to eat. I consulted Chico Rambadi, a local parrot enthusiast. He advised me to give Jacko a whole corncob. To my immense relief Jacko immediately attacked the cob and thereafter settled in nicely.

Mrs. MacIntyre had taught Jacko to speak, but his vocabulary was fairly limited — mostly calls and whistles for Snoopy, the family dog. Nonetheless, his speech was remarkably clear. My sons began to teach him new phrases. Jacko mimicked voices so well that it was always possible to tell which family member had taught him a particular phrase. He was intelligent and inquisitive, always looking for something to do, preferably destructive; this made it difficult to keep him amused. Jacko lived in a large cage that sat on a card table. During the day I would open the cage door and allow him to roam on the outside of his cage as well as on the tabletop. He soon discovered that if he hung upside down from the edge of the table, he could reach the hard cardboard lining on its underside and shred it. For days Jacko methodically attacked this cardboard from all angles until there remained just a small disc in the centre, which was beyond his reach.

AFRICAN GREY PARROT

Parrots are extremely intelligent creatures, rivalled only by members of the Corvid family (crows, ravens, etc.) When Jacko arrived, his feed and water bowls sat on the floor of his cage, a location that I deemed to be unhygienic. I asked my son John to attach the bowls to the side of the cage instead. In no time Jacko had dismantled the attachments, causing the bowls to fall back onto the floor of his cage. John had to devise a much stronger, parrot-proof system of securing the bowls in order to defeat Jacko. During the long daylight hours of summer, I covered Jacko's cage with a blanket at bedtime and secured the cage door with a lock. Without these precautions Jacko would wake at first light, open his cage door and climb on top of his cage. From that vantage point he would make a fearsome racket by practising his repertoire of bells, whistles, catcalls and speech, thereby rousing the entire household. Jacko swiftly learned how to open the lock, so I added a large safety pin in an attempt to strengthen it. He observed closely as I added the safety pin, and most particularly, when I removed it. Two mornings were all he needed: on the third morning he opened the safety pin himself, undid the lock and climbed triumphantly atop his cage.

Jacko had his likes and dislikes, both of people and of objects. Chico Rambadi was at the top of Jacko's 'dislike' list. The mere sound of Chico's voice at the front door would send Jacko into paroxysms of loud squawking — the only time that he ever squawked — for it was Chico who regularly clipped Jacko's flight feathers. Chico would wrap Jacko in a large bath towel for protection from his wicked beak, and then ease out and clip one wing at a time. Jacko loathed both the procedure and its perpetrator. He also preferred some objects over others, as he clearly demonstrated one day. He had previously tossed a cream-coloured peanut dish onto the floor where it had broken. I bought a bright red replacement dish but Jacko despised and shunned it. He adamantly refused to take peanuts from it. I eventually returned the dish to the store and traded it for a cream-coloured one like the original. When Jacko readily accepted the replacement, peace and harmony were restored.

My first adventure with Jacko occurred during his initial summer with me. I had taken him outside onto the lawn to enjoy the fresh air and sunshine. Imagine my consternation when he suddenly lifted off and flew far out over the river! I didn't realize that his flight feathers had grown back to the point where he could fly, albeit somewhat laboriously. This was, after all, a bird that had never flown farther than from his cage to the back of an armchair. I watched with trepidation as Jacko veered across the river, his flight weakening as he steadily lost elevation. I was sure that he would plummet into the water and drown. Fortunately, he just reached the opposite bank of the river where he crash-landed, exhausted, into some bushes at the water's edge. I quickly loaded his cage and a large wooden perching stick into my car in order to retrieve him. I drove rather fast, I confess, for I had to travel several kilometres to reach the nearest bridge, and then backtrack an equal distance on the opposite side of the river. With the help of a friendly cottager, I was able to find Jacko, who was none the worse for wear for his experience. As I carried him across a lawn on his perching stick, he suddenly spread his wings. Fearing that he would take off again, I placed one hand firmly across his back to close his wings and managed to fend off the resulting peck from his powerful beak. Then I popped him into his cage and drove him home.

Jacko made a second flight attempt some months later. He flew from his cage and crashed into the picture window with sufficient force to draw blood. I pondered what to do. The periodic clipping of his flight feathers was a stressful and traumatic procedure for all concerned. Reluctantly, I decided to have him pinioned, a surgical procedure by which the last joint of his wing was removed: the removal of this joint would forever prevent him from flying. Jacko responded well to the surgery and carried on as before, apparently unaffected.

Parrots are naturally musical and can even be taught to sing operatic arias. Jacko was no exception. His great delight was Irish music — an album by the Irish Rovers was a particular favourite. When I played this album, Jacko would dance on top of his cage, shifting his weight from one foot to the other in time with the music. From time to time he would produce small musical phrases and whistles. Sometimes he and I would whistle a duet, first Jacko and then me.

Jacko enjoyed bathing and would signify his desire to bathe by splashing about in his tiny water bowl. When I saw him doing this, I knew that it was time for his 'up up' — a simple phrase that Jacko quickly associated with bathing. He would come out of his cage and clamber up to its top, where I would mist him thoroughly with a plant sprayer. It took quite a long time to wet him enough to satisfy his needs.

One fall evening a deer mouse decided to join us in the living room. It was the time of year when mice start looking for warm shelters. On the first night of the mouse's visit, the little creature managed to steal some of Jacko's birdseed without him noticing. On the second night Jacko saw the thieving mouse and quickly descended from his perch, feathers bristling, to fend off the intruder. I followed the mouse and discovered that it had taken up residence inside the wiring of the electric organ; clearly, it could not stay there. I purchased a live trap, captured the tiny creature and released it into some nearby woodland.

My friend Eve Ticknor suggested that we add a small dead tree to the side of Jacko's cage. She located a suitable trunk from a highway clearance project and brought it over. Jacko was very pleased with the new acquisition and quickly climbed to its highest point by means of beak and talon. From this elevated viewpoint he could see into the garden and observe the activities outside. In winter he would watch for the ducks that waddled across the ice from their patch of open water on the river. If I failed to notice these ducks milling about in the snow waiting to be fed, Jacko would helpfully alert me to their presence with a loud burst of quacking that mimicked the ducks to perfection. One summer day I took the parrot outside and placed him in a small crabapple tree where he surprised me with a hidden explosion of duck quacking.

Jacko was a never-ending source of amusement. He would say "Good-bye!" to us when we went out, and "Hello!" to us when we came in. He was also known to say a rather pointed "Bye-bye!" to visitors when he felt that they had overstayed their welcome. Sometimes it seemed as if there was another person living in the house. I recall the day that I was on my hands and knees under his table cleaning up discarded peanut shells.

"Who are you?" demanded Jacko, repeating one of his pet phrases.

"Jacko, I'm your mother," I replied.

"Wow!" came his delightful response.

Jacko took a great deal of interest in everything that went on around him. From his card table he delighted in lunging for the wagging tail of any passing dog. He would occasionally slide down a leg of the card table, like a fireman descending a pole, and make for our dog Skipper with whom he was always quite willing to roughhouse. Skipper was a large dog, a golden labrador - collie cross, with an exceptionally placid demeanour. He was a gentle giant, friendly with children, with other dogs, and most importantly, with the many young birds that hopped, flitted and flew about my home, especially in nesting season. One day I looked into the living room to see Skipper lying on his tummy with a speckled robin baby perched on each out-stretched foreleg!

Over the years Skipper had put up with frequent advances from Joey, the lovelorn pigeon; he seemed resigned to endure the endless billing and cooing but never engaged the pigeon in play. With Jacko it was different: a typical encounter would begin with the parrot pulling the fur on some part of Skipper's body while he slept. If Skipper did not immediately respond, a second tug would be sure to arouse him. From that point the combatants would jaw with each other throughout an extended skirmish. Sometimes it seemed that half of Jacko's body would be inside Skipper's mouth as they played. One bite would have sent Jacko into eternity, but each participant seemed to respect the other's limits and remarkably, neither party was ever injured.

My faithful parrot helped me in other ways too. When my hearing declined with advancing years, I required a hearing aid but did not always wear it at home. Sometimes I would not hear the telephone ringing. Jacko, ever aware of events in the house, would wait for several rings. If I did not get up, he would render a perfect, and much louder, telephone ring that would alert me to the call.

When I decided that the time had come for me to move into the Orchard View Living Centre, I was faced with the dilemma of what to do with Jacko. Fortunately, I noticed an ad in the local paper by Rosemarie Alves, offering a home to neglected parrots requiring rehabilitation or rescue. Although Jacko did not fall into that category, I gave Rosemarie a call and explained my situation. She came to visit me and kindly agreed to take Jacko. He went to Rosemarie's home, where he joined other parrots and cockatiels. When Rosemarie became ill and had to give up her birds, she found a new owner for Jacko through the Parrot Club. Jacko went to live with a family in Quebec and has learned to speak French. His new owners like to take him camping, which he enjoys very much. Jacko is now 35 years old. May he live to a grand old age.

Chapter 12:
THE GREAT ICE STORM OF 1998

In January of 1998, a perfect storm developed over eastern Ontario, southern Quebec and the northeastern states of New York, Maine, Vermont and New Hampshire. A huge blast of moisture-laden air from the south collided with an Arctic air system from the north, producing ideal conditions for freezing rain. Over the course of three days and two nights, the slow-moving collision dumped as much as seven centimetres of freezing rain, which formed thick coats of ice on every surface. Under the weight of all this ice, power lines snapped; electrical transmission towers buckled; and thousands of trees were felled. Devastation was widespread and comprehensive.

My eldest son John owns 20 hectares of woodland, much of it consisting of second-growth hardwoods like elm, ash and oak. At the peak of the storm, the cacophony of breaking branches and falling trees prevented him from sleeping. He got up in the middle of the night, took his tape recorder and went outside to record the din. To listen to his tape is both frightening and saddening. On his final recording of the night, the noise continues unabated — the thud of falling trees and the snapping of broken branches are woven into the constant crashing and tinkling of falling ice. The cleanup of his property took John more than a year. He was required to build a staggering total of 188 brush piles to clear away all the debris.

SPLINTERED TREE TRUNK
PHOTO BY JOHN LE GEYT

WOODLAND DESTRUCTION
PHOTO BY JOHN LE GEYT

It was much quieter in the Manotick area where I was living. It was not until I arose in the morning that I discovered freezing rain had fallen for the second consecutive night, sheathing the world in a coat of ice. I was relieved to see that my own garden had fared relatively well. The large willow tree had lost half its trunk a few months earlier, but the remaining half held firm, as did the eastern white pines. The small dogwood bush on the riverbank had turned into a spherical ball of ice, perplexing the birds that liked to perch there. The ice on its branches was so thick and slippery that the birds could not maintain their footing. The picnic table that I used as a winter birdfeeder was encrusted with two centimetres of ice: birds were unable to forage. With a bucket of mixed salt and sand that I sprinkled liberally in front of me, I descended the three treacherous steps into the garden and began the arduous task of knocking ice off the picnic table. I then spread a large quantity of birdseed that the birds attacked with great gusto.

I awoke to a house without telephone, and without electricity for the house or the water pump; as a result, I had neither heat nor running water. John's distant home was heated by a wood stove and powered by an electrical generator but I was unable to relocate to it; the roads were impassable due to fallen trees, downed power poles and live electrical wires. My house began to cool. I closed off all the rooms but the living room and drew all the curtains except for one picture window looking toward the river. The freezing rain continued all day, turning the yard into a giant skating rink. I was not entirely alone — I had my two dogs, Jacko the parrot, two budgies and a pair of cockatiels. Together we hunkered down to wait out the storm.

I could not have survived without the generosity of friends. One of my neighbours, Nancy Goth, used her wood stove to heat water and brought me a thermos full each morning. She also lent me four oil lamps, which I placed on the floor at the corners of the card table upon which the parrot's cage sat. I hoped that the rising heat from these lamps would be enough to keep my menagerie of birds alive.

I lit as many candles as I dared — 14 or 15 in all — and burned them day and night. With all the heat sources combined, I managed to maintain that one room at 10 °C, just enough to keep me warm provided that I also wore a sweater and jacket. I quickly ran out of candles and issued an SOS to friends for help — I was amazed by, and grateful to, the number who responded. I learned a lot about candles as I struggled to stay warm in their gentle light. The fat round ones proved to be completely unsatisfactory: their melting candlewax would form a lake that eventually drowned the wick. Tapered candles were much superior but didn't last very long. I placed all the candles inside metal containers — pots, pans, baking dishes and the like — in the hope of preventing the house from burning down while I slept.

Conifer encased in ice
Photo by John Le Geyt

FROZEN BEAUTY
PHOTO BY JOHN LE GEYT

My collection of birds did not appear to be adversely affected by their strange new living conditions. Jacko was his lively self, and the budgies continued to fly about in their diminished airspace. Perhaps they fluffed themselves up a little more at night to deal with the cooler conditions. The first four days after the ice storm were overcast and grey, so it was a relief when the sun finally reappeared. Streaming sunshine warmed the house and began to thaw the smothering ice. I ventured outside, with some trepidation, to shake the trees and bushes in order to liberate them from their icy tombs. The dogs began to move about more freely. Eve Ticknor brought over a one-burner hot plate heated by a fuel canister so that I was able to make tea, warm tinned soup and scramble eggs. A kindly gentleman arrived on my doorstep to lend me a small portable generator for the day; it was sufficiently strong to power the furnace. Suddenly I was too hot and had to throw open the windows to cool off!

Evenings were quiet, peaceful and strangely geared down. I used my portable radio to listen to CFRA, our local radio station, which was a lifeline for keeping us updated on news, information and developments. My supply of candles began to run low. I was now relying on half-burnt candles and the unsatisfactory stubby ones that kept going out. Just when I thought that I would have to beg for more candles, the kitchen light came on, and the refrigerator began humming. Power was restored six days after it had been knocked out.

"Look dogs!" I cried out with delight. "We have power!" (I have always talked to my dogs.)

With the power on, I found everything too bright and too noisy. It was a shock returning to normal living. I think that I may have even suffered a bit of post-traumatic stress. It took several days to recover from this experience before I felt normal again. (I learned later that many others experienced the same feelings.) In due course those of us who remained in our homes were declared 'Survivors of the Ice Storm' and received large, coloured certificates to that effect. Fortunately, my indoor birds all survived unscathed, but I fear that there must have been significant mortality among the wild birdlife as a result of that brutal storm.

Chapter 13:
BIRDING TRIPS AND TOURS

During my working years I was able to travel only briefly within Canada and once to the Florida Everglades, where I saw my first limpkin in Corkscrew Swamp. There I also watched a mother alligator looking after her many tiny babies and marveled at what a good parent she was. Following retirement I had the luxury of more free time and was able to undertake some international travel to view birds in other parts of the world. I was fortunate to have many wonderful experiences in South Africa, Trinidad and Tobago, Costa Rica, Arizona, Britain, Mexico and Grand Manan Island.

SOUTH AFRICA

In 1979 I flew to South Africa to visit my brother David. While there I was asked to give a presentation about Canadian birds to the local birding community in Grahamstown. The secretary of the birding club kindly took me to the local birding hotspots, where I saw so many beautiful birds with very long tails that would billow in every passing breeze. To my mind it seemed that these long feathers would be more of a liability than an asset. My favourite bird in South Africa was the southern red bishop, a brilliant red and black bird of the marshes. It often perched jauntily on top of reeds in the same manner as our red-winged blackbird.

I was fortunate to see a Knysna lourie (also known as Knysna turaco), a crow-sized bird with brilliant green plumage and crowned with a green, white-tipped crest. This lourie was a very active bird that leapt vigorously about in the tree canopy. In flight a Knysna lourie flashes conspicuous scarlet flight feathers — a lovely sight indeed. I also saw a secretary bird, one of Africa's signature species, a bird so unusual that it is classified in a family all by itself.

SECRETARY BIRD
PHOTO BY TONY BECK

With its exceptionally long and elegant black legs, it stands as tall as a heron. Although the secretary bird is an accomplished flier, it prefers to hunt on the ground. With its curious shuffling walk, it can easily travel 30 kilometres a day in search of its prey — snakes, lizards, insects and small mammals, which it dispatches by stamping with its short, sharp talons.

TRINIDAD & TOBAGO

Over the years I made three visits to Trinidad and one to Tobago, where I had my first introduction to tropical birds at the Asa Wright Nature Centre and Lodge. This well-located facility offers exceptional birding and confidently promises 'forty species before breakfast'! From the lodge living room one has an expansive view into the forest, and birdfeeders attract gorgeous hummingbirds, tanagers and motmots. On the first morning our group of birders managed to sight a modest 26 species before lunch.

The Asa Wright property includes a nesting colony of truly unique oilbirds. Their curious name derives from the fact that oilbird chicks were once captured and rendered to yield oil; fortunately, those days have long passed. Oilbirds are large, slim and brownish, with a wingspan approaching one metre. They are strictly nocturnal, sleeping by day in caves and emerging at night to feed on fruits, such as those of the oil palm and tropical laurels. Oilbirds are unique in the world of birds for their ability to navigate using echolocation in the same manner as bats. Because the birds are easily disturbed during their rest periods, the cave entrance at Asa Wright was roped off for their protection. In the dim light of a flashlight, I could see their eyes glowing red inside the darkened cave.

On Trinidad itself the birding highlight of my visit took place at sunset in Caroni Swamp Reserve, one of the largest mangrove wetlands on the island. Each evening scarlet ibis gathered in large numbers for their nightly roost, with some flying in from as far away as the Venezuelan coast, located 11 kilometres away. These imposing, scarlet birds, with their downward curving bills, settled among the trees against the backdrop of the setting sun — it was a stupendous sight. It was not only birders who were in awe of the spectacle: even ordinary tourists would pay for guided tours to see this wondrous event.

SCARLET IBIS
PHOTO BY TONY BECK

My last visit to Caroni Swamp was easily the most memorable. The sky was clear and blue, and our small group filled the sole boat to wait for the ibis. Wave after scarlet wave arrived, settling in the highest part of the island. At the same time the lower reaches of the mangrove forest filled with the egrets, blue herons and tricoloured herons with which the ibis share the island. In the golden afterglow of a brilliant sunset, the sight of so many magnificent birds was truly awe-inspiring — a fitting climax to an almost mystical experience.

COSTA RICA

Costa Rica and Panama are both renowned for the extraordinary richness of their birdlife. I chose Costa Rica because I wished to see the rare resplendent quetzal that can be found in the steamy cloud forest in the mountains above San José. With its spectacular iridescent green plumage and brilliant scarlet breast, this fabled bird is considered one of the world's most beautiful; it will surely be on any birder's 'Most Wanted' list. Sightings of males are especially sought out during mating season when they develop a pair of extraordinarily long tail feathers (up to a metre long) to help them attract a mate.

REPLENDENT QUETZAL
Photo by Saul Bocian

WHITE-THROATED MAGPIE JAY
PHOTO BY SAUL BOCIAN

On our first morning in search of the quetzal, we went up and up, following a twisting dirt track into the Monteverde Cloud Forest Reserve, one of the most ecologically diverse regions of Central America. The great variation of climate, altitude and vegetation in this reserve supports remarkable wildlife including such creatures as jaguar, ocelot, Baird's tapir, three-wattled bellbird, bare-necked umbrellabird and my reclusive target, the resplendent quetzal. On the drive up, my best sighting was of a white-throated magpie jay with its long tail and slightly curving crest. Following lunch at the lodge we drove even higher before being turned back by high winds, but not before seeing a pair of slate-throated redstarts. We descended to San José in the late afternoon, bathed in the golden afterglow of a brilliant crimson sunset.

We returned to Monteverde the next day and hiked along a slippery trail where we caught a glimpse of a pair of quetzals. Unfortunately, the male dived into the undergrowth and disappeared; the female remained perching quietly, and we were able to observe her 'through a glass darkly'. After lunch our group members chose to bird separately. Alone in the forest I was able to see a male quetzal flying away from me with his long tail feathers fluttering behind. The following day we visited a different region and were able to see a rare dove and an emerald toucanet, an olive-green bird with a large yellow and black bill.

The next part of my tour involved a lengthy overland drive southwest to the Osa Peninsula. We left early in the morning in two Land Cruisers and climbed steadily from our 1,300-metre elevation to a pass at 3,000 metres from which we descended a precipitous, winding road almost to sea level. The final 30 kilometres required us to turn off the highway and drive along a rough dirt track that forded no fewer than five streams and rivers. We lurched along in the darkness at about ten kilometres per hour, a most uncomfortable ride made worse by the fact that our driver became so ill that a tour member was forced to take the wheel. The last leg of the journey saw us slipping and sliding up a rutted track along the side of a mountain; finally we arrived, battle-stained and weary, at our destination, Las Ventanas de Osa. This Canadian-owned lodge is Shangri-La itself. The lodge crowns a hill surrounded by undisturbed primeval rainforest, and the land slopes gently toward the Pacific Ocean, offering outstanding views through the trees.

I was awakened very early by the throaty roars of howler monkeys in the forest. Among my first sightings that day were five chestnut-mandibled toucans, which are largely black with canary-yellow faces and upper breasts. Toucans are renowned for the enormous size and extraordinary colouration of their bills. Darwin speculated that the outlandish bills might serve as an attractant to the opposite sex. Others have suggested that they might be used to frighten enemies or intimidate potential rivals. Recent studies have revealed a more compelling explanation: scientists have discovered that toucans can control the flow of blood to these huge lightweight bills, thereby helping to regulate their body temperature. In this respect a toucan's bill has the same function as the ears of an elephant or a hare.

CHESTNUT-MANDIBLED TOUCAN
PHOTO BY SAUL BOCIAN

Other sightings in the forest this day included a slaty-tailed trogon (the male sports a green head, back and breast with a crimson belly and orange bill); a coatimundi (a raccoon-like mammal); and an agouti (a rodent that resembles a guinea pig). When I returned to the lodge for lunch, I glanced skyward and saw orderly formations of frigatebirds and pelicans cruising serenely overhead. Later in the day a group of us went to look at a lek of red-capped manikins. (A lek is a congregation of male birds that gathers together for competitive displays in order to seek an advantage in attracting female partners.) The tiny, spirited manikins, with their black bodies and brilliant red heads, are renowned for their ability to 'moonwalk'; they slide effortlessly back and forth along a branch as if on skates. On our return to the lodge we were surprised to see a black-and-white owl sitting on top of the flagpole set in the lawn. A wonderful day!

I could scarcely believe my eyes the following morning when the first bird that I sighted was a fiery-billed aracari, a large toucan nearly half a metre in length and found only in this corner of Costa Rica. The sexes are similar, with black head and neck, and a bright yellow breast bisected by a broad cummerbund of red across the belly. The lower bill of this handsome creature is black, while the upper bill is fiery red, giving the bird its name. After breakfast we set off in the Land Cruisers to see a colony of boat-billed herons. These unusual birds have large, scoop-like bills and feed nocturnally on fish and shrimp. We also saw several king vultures, some flying and one down on the road. These birds, mostly white with grey-black flight and tail feathers, have the naked heads typical of scavenging vultures. I was thrilled that my Costa Rica birding total now exceeded one hundred species, a target that I had set for myself.

BOAT-BILLED HERON
PHOTO BY SAUL BOCIAN

On the last afternoon at Las Ventanas de Osa, I spent some time observing a few of the other creatures that lived in that beautiful place. First a procession of flower-carrying ants caught my eye. Each tiny insect appeared to be wearing the latest fashion — a tiny, white-flowered hat. Lizards of various sizes darted about the property while one grey specimen lurked on a tree trunk, perfectly camouflaged against the bark. When I approached for a closer look, the lizard, perhaps sensing danger, suddenly raised a striking orange, yellow and white fan in a display of territorial possession. That evening we ate our farewell dinner around a beautifully decorated table, feasting on filet mignon, chicken and assorted vegetables.

The following morning we bade a sad goodbye to the lodge and began the dreadful two-hour drive to Palermo, where we rejoined the paved highway. We climbed once more over the

3,000-metre pass, ate a picnic lunch and returned to San José for the last night. We arose at the ghastly hour of 4:15 a.m., booted and spurred for the return journey to Canada. I arrived home with many wonderful memories of a beautiful country with its friendly people, spectacular birds, lively monkeys and other interesting wildlife.

ARIZONA

When I decided to go birding in Arizona, I went alone, an unusual experience for me as I had always travelled with a conducted tour. I flew to Tucson, rented a car and drove to the southwest corner of Arizona near the Mexican border at Nogales. In this region of the state, towering mountains rise abruptly from the desert lowlands. Desert plants, such as prickly pear, saguaro cactus and ocotillo, give way rapidly to sycamores, oaks and pines with increasing elevation and decreasing temperatures.

Known locally as the Sky Islands, these mountains offer exceptional diversity in plant, animal and birdlife. The canyons that have been carved into the flanks of these mountains offer particularly rich birding opportunities. In the lowlands one of my first sightings was a phainopepla, a member of the Silky Flycatcher family. Both sexes are crested and have red eyes, the male being glossy black and the female, a dull grey. I was also pleased to see a Gambel's quail and a cactus wren, the largest member of the Wren family in North America.

On the drive south from Tucson, I stopped to visit Colossal Cave, a cavern nearly 50 kilometres in length; its meandering clefts and hollows have never been fully explored. Dripping stalactites hung from the roof, their length attesting to the great age of the cave. The 100-kilometre drive south produced some startling scenery — speckled dry hills, jumbles of pink boulders, and fields of shimmering, silvery grass. It was extremely windy, sending dry tumbleweeds bowling across the landscape in a scene reminiscent of countless Western movies.

I reached my destination, Cave Creek, and was assigned a stone cottage with large sliding doors. The creek splashed down a waterfall at the rear of the property — it was a lovely place and so very different from anything that I had ever seen in my life. A blue-throated hummingbird zoomed past to sip sugar water from a nearby feeder. I also saw an acorn woodpecker, a bird that drills countless rows of holes and then carefully fills them with acorns for the winter. During my time at Cave Creek, my sightings included several Mexican (formerly grey-breasted) jays, Audubon warblers, a male ruby-crowned kinglet, various sparrows, a jackrabbit with enormous ears, a bunny and four greater roadrunners. The roadrunners were much larger than I had anticipated. Speedy roadrunners have been clocked running in excess of 30 km/h. They are opportunistic feeders and will eat almost anything that they can catch — insects, rodents, small birds, spiders, lizards and even rattlesnakes.

My next destination was Mile Hi Ranch, located near the border town of Douglas. En route I saw what may have been the highlight of the Arizona trip — the most enormous flock of yellow-headed blackbirds, Brewer's blackbirds, red-winged blackbirds and cowbirds. Huge numbers would rise from the fields like a vast swarm of bees, while others took communal baths in large puddles. Along the banks of the San Pedro River I saw a lark sparrow, an Abert's towhee and my first vermilion flycatcher, gloriously red with black wings — a more brilliant red than that of a scarlet tanager. Later I saw three more males as well as several females with their pearl-coloured sides.

Upon arriving at Mile Hi, I was surprised to find that I had arrived a day early for my reservation, which I had booked myself. Fortunately a cabin was available, and I spent one night there before relocating to the one that had been set aside for me. Mile Hi Ranch, now operated by the Nature Conservancy, has a lush evergreen forest, a babbling brook and well-appointed cabins. As I walked up a trail before breakfast, I caught a glimpse of a painted redstart, a canyon wren and a Strickland's woodpecker. Farther along the trail I discovered a Hutton's vireo building a nest in a small tree. Each afternoon it was possible to visit the nearby Lehzers' Ranch and observe the birds at their feeders — it was a great show. There I saw four species of towhee, a pair of gila woodpeckers, Gambel's and scaled quail, mourning and white-winged doves, and white-crowned sparrows.

After my stay at Mile Hi, I relocated to Madera Canyon, where my cabin had its own hummingbird feeder. I had barely settled in when a hummingbird with a red bill appeared at the feeder — it was a broad-billed hummingbird, a new species for me. This is a lovely bird; males sport a metallic, dark-green back and breast, a deep-blue throat and red bill. I descended from the heights the next day to visit the Sonora Desert Museum. It was very hot, and I didn't like to see so many creatures in cages. The large aviary was a bit better as it was large enough to permit free flight for the birds. It allowed me to have a close-up view of many of the Arizona birds that I had only seen at a distance. At the end of the day it was good to retreat to my cool, quiet home in Madera Canyon. I went looking for a black-shouldered kite in the grasslands the following day and surprised myself by finding one sitting in a tree. This falcon-like raptor, whitish with black shoulder epaulets, is uncommon — an exciting find. My last significant sightings in Arizona included a pair of western bluebirds and two pygmy nuthatches.

GRAND CANYON
PHOTO BY MICHAEL LE GEYT

Following my excursions in southern Arizona, I drove to Phoenix to meet up with my long-time friend, Florence Boyd. Together we joined a bus tour to visit the Grand Canyon, a 'must see' for any visitor to Arizona. We arrived at the canyon on a sunny day in the late afternoon. The marvelous sunset made for ideal viewing conditions: the waning rays of the setting sun brought out the extraordinarily rich colours of the canyon walls and crags. We arose early, hoping to see the sun rise over the canyon, but were dismayed to find cloudy conditions and falling snow. Nonetheless, we caught glimpses of the fantastic canyon and were grateful that we had seen it in all its glory on the previous day.

Britain

In 1978, twenty-six years after emigrating from Britain, I returned to my country of birth with a birding and sightseeing tour called 'The Great British Experience'. It was an extensive tour, looping around the British Isles in a great, counterclockwise sweep. I found that Britain had greatly changed. Huge motorways spanned the country; new construction was under way in towns and cities; and everything was very expensive. We departed from London by coach for the Norfolk coast, stopping along the way to visit the nesting site of two pairs of extremely rare Eurasian stone-curlews. We were greatly distressed the following morning to learn that one of the pairs had been caught by a fox during the night, a blow to a vanishing species that is nearing extinction.

We headed for the Cley Marshes Nature Reserve with its ponds, pools and scrapes, located along the Norfolk coast. With blinds and hides for birders, this is one of Britain's premier birding locations. We first saw the scarce and secretive Garganey duck (the male has a brown head, speckled breast and a wide crescent of white above the eye); a Eurasian serin (the smallest European member of the Finch family — a small, stripy bird with patches of yellow, somewhat similar to the North American pine siskin); and a woodchat shrike, an especially good sighting. This tiny but ferocious hunter is a striking black and white with a chestnut head.

We struck out northward, passing through Lincoln on the way to lovely Durham Cathedral, my favourite church in all of Britain. The tour continued with a brief stop at Hadrian's Wall followed by a short visit to the nesting site of a pair of black-necked grebes. We then made for Bamburgh, the departure point for the Farne Islands, those idyllic islands of my youth. Fifteen to twenty islands a few kilometres offshore, mostly low-lying but several with rocky cliffs, are roughly divided into inner and outer groups. In medieval times various monks and hermits retreated to the islands in search of peace and tranquility. One of these, Saint Aidan, made the first recorded mention of the islands in 651 AD. Another, Saint Cuthbert, is noted for issuing a proclamation in 676 AD that protected the eider ducks and other nesting seabird species. This edict is thought to be the first bird protection law in history. Saint Cuthbert would be pleased to know that the entire island group has now been declared a bird sanctuary. Human traffic is restricted to a very small area with well-defined pathways. A total of 230 species have been recorded on the islands over the centuries, including the great auk, which was observed there before becoming extinct in the 1760s.

In 1979 an Aleutian tern made a two-day visit to the Farne Islands, the sole recorded European sighting of this species. How an Alaskan bird arrived there is a complete mystery. One lesser-crested tern, dubbed Elsie, came to the Farne Islands every summer from 1984 until 1997. She paired with a male sandwich tern, and they produced several broods of hybrid offspring during this period. Lesser-crested terns usually nest on islands off the Mediterranean coast of Libya and migrate to the west coast of Africa in winter. It is anyone's guess why Elsie returned to the Farnes for all those years. In June of 1982 a fledgling Arctic tern was banded in its nest on the islands. Just three months later the same bird was sighted 22,000 kilometres away in Melbourne, Australia — one of the longest journeys by any bird ever recorded. An estimated quarter-million seabirds — black-legged kittiwakes, northern gannets, European shags, greater cormorants, Atlantic puffins and terns — now nest annually on the Farne Islands. This is a much larger number than in my youth and a testament to excellent management by the National Trust.

We continued our tour northward, heading for the small town of Aviemore in Scotland's Cairngorms National Park. En route we saw a common greenshank, a golden plover and three endangered black grouse. We arrived at an enormous 400-room hotel, which was very comfortable and full of modern conveniences, but its huge scale seemed better suited to North America than to Scotland. From our base in Aviemore we began to explore the surrounding area, albeit with some difficulty as our coach was really too large for the narrow, winding roads. On one occasion our driver had to reverse more than a kilometre to allow a large truck to pass. At Loch Vaa we were pleased to see a Slavonian grebe; with its black head and golden ear tufts, it is considered Britain's most attractive grebe. Other sightings included grey wagtail, ring ouzel, peregrine falcon and an immature golden eagle.

We departed the next day, travelling along the length of a great sea loch, Loch Duich, bound for the Isle of Skye in the Inner Hebrides. This is such a lovely part of Scotland with ruggedly beautiful peaks of the Cuillen Mountains on one flank and seaward views to the south toward the curiously named islands of Rum, Eigg and Muck. From Skye we crossed by ferry to the Outer Hebrides — the islands of North and South Uist, Benbecula and Barra — which have a stark, rugged charm of their own. These treeless, barren islands, carved by lochs and lochans, are dotted with sturdy, whitewashed homes and grazed by countless thousands of sheep.

We drove first around North Uist to a birding reserve where we wandered blissfully through meadows filled with wildflowers — daisies, buttercups and small, yellow pansies. We ended the day with an elegant evening meal of lentil soup, jugged hare and raspberry pavlova. Our tour through Scotland continued with a short ferry ride to South Uist, where we experienced a frustrating search for corncrakes. We could hear the calls of these secretive and elusive members of the Rail family, but they remained maddeningly hidden. That evening we slept aboard the ferry MV *Glaymore* in preparation for the next day's crossing to Oban on the mainland. We departed early in the morning, sailing down the Little Minch, the strait that separates the islands of Skye and South Uist, and enjoyed sightings of seabirds and whales along the way. The largest gannet colony in Britain is located in this region of Scotland.

Upon arrival in the handsome city of Oban, we visited a magnificent baronial manor house surrounded by stunning displays of rhododendrons and foxgloves. During a short walk I saw my first wood warbler as well as a goldcrest, a tiny bird very similar to the North American golden-crowned kinglet. We awoke to rain the next day and drove along the length of Loch Lomond, wreathed in mist, before passing through Glasgow on our way south, heading for the Lake District of northwest England. En route we drove through Ambleside, where I had attended teacher's college (now re-named Charlotte Mason College in honour of its founder) so many years earlier. I was pleased to see that the original college building was still standing, albeit surrounded by many newer structures. We also visited nearby Rydal Water, where Wordsworth lived and wrote his famous poem to the lovely little daffodils that still thrive there. Along the way I saw signposts to many familiar place names of my youth — it was all very nostalgic.

We carried on southward and crossed into Wales, staying at Aber in a delightful little hotel called Tan-y-Fyn. Here we saw roseate terns, and in what was the highlight of the trip for me, a colony of choughs. Choughs have a tiny range in Britain and can be found in just a few locations on the coast of Wales. These large black birds of the Corvid family have red feet and curving red bills. We witnessed an adult feeding its large fledgling and later saw both parents and offspring in flight. At Conwy Castle

I marvelled at the massive defensive walls surrounding the imposing medieval castle, which was so well preserved that it might have been built yesterday. In fact this fortress was built in an extraordinary burst of activity between 1283 and 1287 AD. I climbed to the top of one of the castle turrets and had a wonderful view of the surrounding countryside. We left Conwy looking for hen harriers and red kites along twisting roads lined with hedgerows. Red kites are rufous-coloured raptors with forked tails. They are more common in continental Europe than in Britain; we were fortunate to see five of them. They scavenge as well as hunt small mammals, birds, insects and even earthworms. Unfortunately, their scavenging habit puts them at risk of poisoning from eating tainted carcasses.

The tour carried on through the Cotswolds, the Roman town of Bath and on to Stonehenge, which was very crowded but stunning nonetheless. My birthday fell on one of these days, and I was fêted with a rousing version of 'Happy Birthday' when I came down to breakfast. Sightings on these days included a Dartford warbler (a grey warbler with a long tail, the male with rufous breast and sides); a woodlark (famous for its melodious song as it flies in an upward spiral); a hawfinch (a bulky, bull-headed finch); and a willow tit (which resembles a chickadee and is now in serious decline in Britain). I left Britain with some degree of sadness but with wonderful memories of this beautiful country with its great heritage and interesting birds. It will be long remembered.

MEXICO

In 1990 I decided to take a WINGS Birding Tour to Mexico. The company had briefly suspended tours there because of violence associated with the drug trade. The situation had since calmed down, and the company was keen to re-establish its tour activities. Evidently not all birders were convinced that the area was safe. When I was informed that the tour was not selling well, I expected that it would be cancelled. Imagine my surprise when I discovered that the tour would proceed, and that I would be its sole member! So it was that a solitary 76-year old birder from Canada was met at the airport in Mazatlán by a young man in his thirties. Jeff Kingery would be my guide for the tour. He had been raised in Mexico and spoke fluent Spanish, which would prove to be an asset at the frequent police roadblocks that we would encounter. Even better, he would be bringing his $2,000 telescope. With this wonderful telescope and Jeff's superb birding knowledge, I would see birds like I had never seen them before.

Our first destination was San Blas, a four-hour drive to the south along a narrow road crowded with smelly diesel trucks belching black exhaust. There I was particularly thrilled to see painted buntings. The male of this species — with its dark blue head, lime green back, red breast and rump — is often referred to as 'the most beautiful North American bird'. We also saw a blue grosbeak, a Sinaloa wren and many parrots before taking the obligatory afternoon siesta — a wonderful practice from my point of view.

We resumed birding at the local sewage lagoon in late afternoon. A sewage lagoon will no doubt be an unappealing destination for a non-birder. Experienced birders, on the other hand, know that the rich organic matter of such a lagoon sustains a wealth of insect larvae that hatch into midges, crane flies, mosquitoes and gnats. Both larvae and insects provide an abundant food source that attracts shorebirds and waterfowl, which in turn attract raptors. During our visit we were rewarded by sighting black-necked stilts (with very long, bright-red legs) and two crane hawks (grey with black and white tails, and long legs that they use to extract prey from holes and crevices). On this occasion though, the hawks were hunting for lizards in the crowns of coconut palms.

One morning Jeff and I witnessed an enormous flock of red-winged blackbirds leaving their roost to feed, a sight that resembled a great horde of frenzied locusts. We were also intrigued to watch more than a hundred vultures soaring upward on a huge thermal and then dispersing to all quarters in their gliding search for food. Like cormorants, vultures often sit and sunbathe to warm up, a practice that also serves to deter parasites within their feathers.

Later we took a four-hour boat trip that began along a river where pelicans and cormorants were roosting in trees. Eventually we entered a mangrove swamp, an eerie environment in which the salt-resistant mangroves march into the ocean by dropping down new roots from their branches. We returned home in the dark with Jeff using a flashlight to pick out the red eyes of the potoos. This fascinating and unusual bird, related to nightjars and frogmouths, consists of several species in a family of their own. Potoos are strictly nocturnal and mainly eat insects, flying out from their perches like flycatchers. Their call consists of five mournful, descending notes with the first two louder than the following three. During the day potoos sleep upright, typically on a tree stump of similar, mottled brown colouration, so that they simply appear to be an extension of the stump.

Our last evening visit to the sewage lagoons had a treat in store — twenty bright-green Mexican parrotlets, with blue rumps and blue primary feathers, feeding on seedheads. Half a dozen parrotlets were gathered in a smaller group, engaged in mutual preening. I was also pleased to discover a russet-crowned motmot in the forest. This striking bird has a bluish-green back with an orange-brown cap and sports a blue tail that is as long as its body. When hunting, motmots sit patiently waiting for small invertebrates and large insects; occasionally, they feed on fruit.

The next phase of our Mexican adventure took us into the Sierra Madre Mountains along the Durango Highway, a beautifully engineered road with marvellous views. We stayed at La Villa Bianca, a German-run hotel with the most extraordinary collection of bric-à-brac — assorted china, garish pictures, old tools, dried flowers, bundles of sticks and misshapen gourds. On this leg of the trip we hoped to see tufted jays, which are very rare and found locally only in this part of Mexico. We rose early in the morning and began our birding in an open area with scattered shrubs, pines and oaks. Our first sighting was of a pair of bumblebee hummingbirds at play. These tiny hummers, with males sporting an iridescent reddish-purple throat, are the second smallest of their species; only Cuba's bee hummingbird is smaller. We added another 26 species that day, but alas — no tufted jays. Our luck changed the next morning with the sudden appearance of that stunningly beautiful bird, which Jeff attracted from the forest by playing its calls on a tape recorder. The tufted jay is a patchy black and white bird with its head topped by a fringed crest. This crest is highly mobile and can be raised and lowered at will in times of excitement or aggression. Like all jays, tufted jays are active and raucous, calling noisily to each other as they forage and cavort.

On the return drive to Mazatlán our sightings included titmice; military macaws (with iridescent green bodies, red facial patches, blue flight feathers and red tails edged with blue); and yellow grosbeaks. We also saw a sparkling-tailed hummingbird; both sexes have forked and banded tails with the greenish males having bluish-purple throats, while the duller females have cinnamon underparts. Later we spotted a laughing falcon, so named because its call resembles maniacal laughter, especially when disturbed.

On the drive to the airport, Jeff and I reminisced about our two-week tour together.

"You must have been alarmed," I offered, "when you saw an old woman in her seventies tottering along with a walking stick."

He chuckled and replied, "I always hope for the best!"

In fact the two of us got along exceedingly well, despite the great age difference. We were both madly keen birders, eager to rise early in the morning and get going. Neither of us required coffee, a fact that delighted Jeff.

"It's often very difficult to make an early start with a large group," he explained. "You can only move as fast as the slowest member."

We were both happy to grab a quick bite in the local market for breakfast or lunch — birding was always our first priority. At our final parting in Los Angeles airport, we hugged and wished each other well with heartfelt sincerity.

GRAND MANAN ISLAND

Grand Manan Island is located in the Bay of Fundy between the provinces of Nova Scotia and New Brunswick. Long renowned as a birding hotspot (more than 350 species have been recorded), the island lies along the Atlantic flyway of migrating birds. In September of 1996 I went there on a birding tour led by Tony Beck, a highly knowledgeable birding authority to whom I regularly turned for assistance when writing my bird column for the Ottawa *Citizen*.

The tour began with flights to New Brunswick via Halifax. We then drove to Black's Harbour, from where the ferry leaves for Grand Manan Island. Whitecaps whipped the ocean surface, and a cold wind cut into us. It was an inauspicious beginning made even more ominous by the weather forecast. The stormy remnants of Hurricane Edouard were sweeping up the Atlantic coast, bringing high seas, tidal surges and gusty winds. The weather was still fair on our first full day on the island, but unfortunately the tide was out midday, and the seabirds were far from land. The Bay of Fundy has some of the world's highest tides — when the tide is out, it is well and truly out!

The leading edge of the hurricane arrived that night, bringing pelting rain and impossible birding conditions. Of necessity we sheltered at our hotel, the Marathon Inn, while the storm raged. I played several games of Scrabble with Bonnie, another tour member, in front of a roaring fireplace. The hurricane winds increased that night and blew strongly throughout the following day accompanied by stinging rain. As birding was out of the question, Tony arranged alternative activities. In the morning we visited the local museum and looked at the specimens of stuffed birds, some tired and dusty. In the afternoon we visited the local fish-processing plant where herring were filleted, smoked and packed. One of the friendly workers gave us a small sample of the finished product to taste — very salty! Along the seashore beside the plant we saw a large flock of semipalmated sandpipers and semipalmated plovers, which alternately flashed their dark backs and white underparts as they wheeled and turned in massed flight. Next we went to see the lobster pens where the creatures were corralled with their big claws tied until needed — not a happy place.

Hurricane Edouard blew through that night, and we were greeted with blue skies and a return to warm weather the following day. Our group was taken out into the bay aboard a lobster boat, the MV *Breezy Sea*, to view seabirds and look for right whales. These slow-moving leviathans of the ocean are gentle giants, second only to blue whales in size. They prefer to live in near-shore waters like continental shelves, coastal bays and inlets, where their preferred foods can be found in abundance. North Atlantic right whales earned the name 'right' from whalers who coveted them for their high blubber content. Not only did this blubber yield large amounts of oil but its buoyancy also prevented a dead whale from sinking.

Nowadays with a moratorium on the hunting of right whales, their greatest threat is from collisions with large, ocean-going vessels. We were fortunate to find a group of right whales engaged in a courting display of awesome power. The sea was roiled by the thrashing of these great creatures — a maelstrom of flippers, splotchy heads and tail flukes as the attendant males jostled mightily in their attempt to mate with a sole female. It was impossible to say just how many whales were present in the writhing mass.

Shearwaters skimmed the ocean surface around us on our boat trip; they often accompany whales and look for fish stirred up by them. These medium-sized seabirds, with very long wings, are especially long-lived. They come ashore only to breed and raise their offspring inside excavated burrows. When we returned to Grand Manan Island, we went looking for shore-birds but were frustrated by two young girls walking along the shore ahead of us. Little did they realize that their innocent stroll was scaring off the birds before we could identify them.

The next day we boarded the MV *Breezy Sea* once more and headed south of Grand Manan Island through a maze of rocky islets. We saw two whales — a fin and a humpback — as well as an immature bald eagle and harbour seals. Our skipper had brought along a bucket of chum, remnants of herring from the smokehouse, in order to draw in nearby seabirds. He scattered these fishy bits and pieces into the sea, and in no time at all, we were besieged by gulls, shearwaters and gannets. I mar-velled how many seemed to appear out of thin air when none had been visible previously. The shearwaters were especially impressive as they skimmed the surface of the water, collecting fish morsels at the speed of light. All this frenzied activity took place against a clear blue sky and was definitely one of the tour highlights.

The challenges of this trip, ranging from howling winds and driving rain to sauntering little girls, served to remind me that birding trips do not always go as planned, regardless of the skill and knowledge of the leader. At times like this, one must be prepared to go with the flow and accept an altered itinerary; if not, one can become very frustrated. It was on this tour that I felt my advancing years catch up to me; at 82 years of age, I was too exhausted to accompany the group on its final day of birding. I had to accept that this would be my last birding tour. When I recall all the wonderful birds that I have been able to see in my travels over the years, I consider myself very fortunate indeed. While I no longer have the physical mobility to travel, the highlights of those wonderful trips — the stunning beauty of the scarlet ibis, the billowing tail feathers of the incomparable resplendent quetzal, the wondrous bill of the fiery-billed aracari — remain etched in my memory and continue to give me great pleasure.

Chapter 14:
RETIREMENT AT ORCHARD VIEW LIVING CENTRE

. . . .

In October 2000 at the age of 86, I decided that the time had come for me to sell my house and move into a retirement home. I chose the recently opened Orchard View Living Centre (OVLC), located 15 kilometres south of Ottawa near Manotick Station. In its promotional literature the facility was described as a 'home away from home' rather than as an institution, and this appealed to me. The new building was set on ten hectares of rolling land largely encircled by forest. It was surrounded by foundation plantings of shrubs and Amur maples as well as a scattering of young conifers and locust trees.

Living at the OVLC has proven very much to my liking. For a person like me who has lived nearly all her life in a rural location, its pastoral setting is ideal. My room on the ground floor has a large window, one half of which opens on a ratchet; it faces northeast, and so I receive goodly amounts of morning sun. Beneath this window I have a semi-circular flowerbed centred on a small Amur maple; there I can grow many plants attractive to hummingbirds. I have placed several birdfeeders and suet logs in the collection of small trees outside my window. Thanks to the strategic placement of these feeders, I can view them all simultaneously. With my declining mobility, birdwatching from my window has become my principal pastime.

ELIZABETH FLANKED BY OVLC OWNER ROSALIA PRINCIOTTA AND PRESIDENT JOE PRINCIOTTA
PHOTO BY FEMMY WRIGHT

The OVLC has a collection of pet animals as well — fallow deer, llamas and once, a reindeer named Rudolph. I used to feed these animals when I was able to go out for afternoon walks. Rudolph loved bananas. I would first peel a banana and give him the fruit. Then I would give him the peel, which he would suction into his mouth like a piece of spaghetti. I always took friends down to meet Rudolph so that they could be entertained by his eating antics. Rudolph was lonely, and so a mate was found for him. This doe was discovered to be pregnant soon after her arrival, and in due course she delivered a white stag baby. He grew into a magnificent specimen and became the dominant male; Rudolph was clearly afraid of him. The stag would chase Rudolph away when we went to feed them both. One winter Rudolph was found in his paddock with a badly broken leg. Sadly, there was no alternative but to euthanize him. Suspicion naturally fell on the white stag but no proof could be established.

The limited plantings of shrubs and small trees offered little shelter protection for birds in my early years at the OVLC. To assist in attracting greater numbers, I immediately put up two feeders outside my window. Gradually the birds began to come, beginning with black-capped chickadees. When I put up hanging logs containing a mix of suet and birdseed, I attracted both hairy and downy woodpeckers. It was a long, potentially dangerous flight from the surrounding forest to my feeders. The birds were very exposed during these flights, and I was concerned for their safety.

A resident pair of Cooper's hawks was well established and had nested around the OVLC for years. These fast and agile hawks are crow-sized, and they feed primarily on smaller birds. One year they raised two magnificent offspring, which hunted all summer at the far end of the property near a tiny pond. I feel certain that the fledgling eastern bluebirds and tree swallows, both of which emerged from nestboxes near the pond, did not escape the clutches of these ruthlessly efficient predators. By the end of the summer there were no small birds remaining around the pond. To make matters worse, a pair of common crows also nested nearby. Crows steal eggs and eat nestling birds of other species. With such efficient predators hunting in the immediate vicinity, it was hardly surprising that most small birds stayed away. It was a worrying beginning.

Soon after I moved into the OVLC, four cedar trees were planted halfway between my feeders and the surrounding forest. These additions proved beneficial for they allowed the forest birds to make a safer, stepwise journey to my feeders. American goldfinches and chipping sparrows began to visit regularly during the summer. The Cooper's hawks continued to nest in the area for a period, but one year they failed to appear. Their absence, combined with the continued growth of the trees and shrubs, encouraged increasing diversification of the birdlife.

DOWNY WOODPECKER
PHOTO BY CALVIN D. HANSON

My woodpeckers raised their families in the forest and took food from my suet logs back to their offspring. When the youngsters were fledged, their father (identifiable as a male by the red patch on his head, in contrast to the female, which lacks this mark) would bring them, one by one, to my feeding station. On the first visit they would arrive together at the Amur maple. Then the father would fly to the suet log, collect food and return to feed his youngster. On the second day they would fly directly to the log, where the father would again feed the youngster. By the third day the father declined to feed the youngster. The message was quite clear: 'There's the log; there's the food; feed yourself!' Interestingly the female woodpecker never appeared at my feeding station. Perhaps she was involved in showing alternative feeding stations to her offspring or teaching them to locate natural food sources.

Year after year both hairy and downy woodpeckers brought their young families to my feeders, with the result that the more recent arrivals are now extremely tame and well-habituated to the activities of the OVLC residents. The forest is also home to large pileated woodpeckers — spectacular, crow-sized birds with flaming red crests. They have a distinctive loud call, and the undersides of their wings flash white in flight. They were once a rare sight but their population increased significantly with the arrival of Dutch elm disease, which killed off many large trees that then became suitable for nesting cavities. I wondered if these giant woodpeckers might ever pay a visit to my feeders.

I was sitting in the garden under a gazebo one day when, to my great pleasure, I spied a male pileated woodpecker hanging from the feeder log. At first I presumed that he was feeding himself, but after filling his enormous beak, he flew to a nearby locust tree and began to feed a fledgling hanging quietly on its trunk. This particular locust tree also contained a feeder of sunflower seeds that were popular with the red squirrels. With the young woodpecker still in the tree, a squirrel arrived and began to climb the trunk. To my surprise this young woodpecker, barely out of its nest hole, flew down out of the tree with its white under-feathers flashing and chased the squirrel away. Moments later the squirrel cautiously returned but was again repelled. After a further half-dozen futile attempts, the squirrel conceded defeat and hopped away to forage elsewhere. In the following days the two pileated woodpeckers returned to the feeder log and followed the training procedure well-established by the hairy and downy woodpeckers: Day 1: Feed youngster in Amur maple tree; Day 2: Feed youngster on log; Day 3: Youngster, feed yourself!

Summertime became a hive of activity at my feeding station with all these woodpecker families. Lovely rose-breasted grosbeaks, which nested in the forest, brought their young family too. Chickadee parents, with as many as five or six youngsters in tow, were reliable visitors. White-breasted nuthatch families were frequent callers, and once the less common red-breasted nuthatch dropped by. When the white-breasted nuthatch family arrived, the young ones were already well developed and highly mobile. Like their parents, they ran up and down tree trunks headfirst. At one point they flitted to the windowsill and peered inside my room with considerable curiosity. Later they flew up to the transom above my window, where they huddled together to survey the feeding scene below.

Noisy blue jay families were also commonplace. The arrival of the predatory jays would make the smaller birds very wary, and they would be sure to keep their distance. The blue jay fledglings were the most raucous of the young birds visiting my feeders. They screeched incessantly for food and required the longest period of parental feeding before they became weaned.

Perhaps the most remarkable callers to my suet log were white-winged crossbills, a species of finch usually found in the boreal forests of northern Canada. The males of this species are rosy-pink with black wings and prominent white wing bars;

the females are a dull olive-grey with similar wing patterns. The overlapping mandibles of the crossbill allow it to specialize in feeding on cones that other birds cannot open. I had an excellent view of them as they fed on the suet log just outside my window with their spectacular plumage gleaming in the afternoon sun. I regret that these white-winged crossbills made just a single visit. I hope that they will return and bring red crossbills with them. I recently had a visit from another member of the Finch family, a male purple finch. Such a lovely bird, a small, stripy sparrow-sized bird with the male looking as if he has been dipped in raspberry juice. Unfortunately, his visit was rather fleeting because he was scared away by the racket of tree pruners working nearby.

The population levels of some species have changed significantly at the OVLC over the years due to factors such as predation and habitat loss. Plump mourning doves were once quite common but no more: they were a favourite target of the Cooper's and sharp-shinned hawks. Somewhat surprisingly the numbers of American robins have declined too. In my early years at the OVLC there were as many as six nesting pairs, but most recently just a single pair succeeded in raising a family. Another pair did build a nest in a spruce tree near my room for two years in succession, but both years the nest was abandoned. I suspect that crows discovered the nest and wreaked havoc on the eggs.

As the trees and shrubs grew up around the property, the terrain became less favourable for the eastern bluebirds, which prefer open fields and grasslands. With regular lawn mowing, the tall grass that once existed is now gone, along with the insects that sheltered there and formed much of the diet for bluebirds. Nonetheless, one pair did manage to breed successfully, and this pleased me. The numbers of tree swallows have also declined in line with the global decrease in swallow populations. I was very happy when one pair recently selected a nestbox near the pond and successfully raised a brood.

A STRUTTING WILD TURKEY TOM DISPLAYS MAGNIFICENT FORM.
PHOTO BY CALVIN D. HANSON

On the positive side, the reappearance of the wild turkey has been most welcome. Wild turkeys were once commonplace throughout eastern North America, but hunting and habitat loss drastically reduced their numbers. In recent years conservation efforts and hunting restrictions have helped the turkey population rebound dramatically. Turkeys have even been successfully introduced into areas of Canada and the U.S. where they were not indigenous. Male turkeys (called toms) forage and roost together in the winter; female turkeys (called hens) also live communally but apart from the males, more typically in the forest where they nest and raise their chicks. Males are much larger than females — a large male can easily exceed a metre in height. Males have bare red heads, red throats and red wattles. In breeding season their feathers are gloriously coloured with a mixture of bronze, copper, red, purple, green and orange iridescence. Turkeys are omnivorous, and the nuts of many trees — oaks, hazels, butternuts, chestnuts and hickories — are favoured foods. Seeds, berries, roots and insects form part of their diet as well as small amphibians, snakes and lizards.

The return of turkeys to my area was heralded by a memorable event that I like to call 'The Winter of the Wild Turkeys'. I was sitting in my reclining armchair on a winter day when I experienced that disquieting feeling that one gets when one is being watched. I turned toward the window, where my gaze was met by one from an ugly, prehistoric-looking head — it belonged to a large turkey! I got up slowly and looked outside to see that there were three toms feeding on the seed scattered on the ground. In subsequent weeks this flock of tom turkeys steadily increased until there were about 30 of them coming to my feeders. They would venture out from the forest and descend over what I like to call 'The Great Wall of China'. This 'wall' is in fact a very long garden bed constructed of brickwork and raised so that wheelchair-bound residents can cultivate flowers and vegetables from a sitting position.

When the turkeys assembled under my window to feed on the seed spillage, there would be a sea of shiny metallic backs glinting in the sunshine. Every now and then a rather primitive-looking head would lift up. We would be eyeball to eyeball just a few metres apart with only the window separating us. As the winter progressed, the tom turkeys became quite tame. I noted how much attention the flock paid to its leader. If this dominant tom decided to return to the forest, the others would be sure to follow. Although turkeys can fly short distances if pressed, their normal evasive action is to run away. If anything frightened my birds, they would dash away on their powerful legs, leap over 'The Great Wall of China', and disappear into the forest.

When the days lengthened into spring, the toms developed their courting plumage. The red colouration of their heads and necks steadily intensified, spreading down onto their breasts; every day they became more handsome. One day a tom began to practice his courtship display on the lawn in front of my window. With feathers fluffed, tail spread in a huge elegant fan and wings sagging, he strutted up and down, all the while gobbling softly. His courting plumage was indescribably beautiful as the light illuminated his glossy feathers. Later in the day a female turkey mysteriously appeared; she was the first that I had seen all winter. Where had she been hiding? Had she been drawn to the tom by the sound of his gobbling? In no time at all, the tom approached the hen and renewed his courting display, but she disdained his advances. With the advent of spring my flock of toms gradually filtered away. I was hoping that the turkeys would re-appear the following winter, but that was not to be. Instead I was visited by a solitary male. He became a regular visitor but remained alone the entire winter.

As the years have progressed, my birdwatching has been mostly out of my window, around the building and at a small pond in the Tony Princiotta Memorial Park (named in honour of the OVLC founder). This park consists of a small, oval pond with an island in the middle. To reach this pond I would walk along the length of the residences. One summer two pairs of cliff swallows built their elongated mud nests under the eaves of the building. I was admiring their handiwork when I noticed a white-breasted nuthatch working its way along the brickwork, looking for grubs, spiders and insects in the cracks. Chickadees and even squirrels commonly scoured the brickwork cracks as well. On this particular day a large moth was resting peacefully under a windowsill as the nuthatch worked ever closer. I held my breath as the nuthatch approached. It suddenly spied the large moth, and in a split second, impaled the tasty morsel with its powerful, upswept bill. It then flew off triumphantly to feed its family.

I was witness to a number of murders over the years — especially of pigeons and mourning doves killed by the Cooper's hawks. A most unexpected attack came the day that a crow attacked a juvenile pileated woodpecker. These two birds are approximately the same size, and the pileated woodpecker has a large, powerful beak. Both factors made it an unlikely target for a crow. The woodpecker was returning to the forest when the crow swooped down from above and knocked it to the ground. The crow would likely have killed its target had it not been for Andy Higgs, the OVLC maintenance manager, who intervened to fend off the crow. The pileated woodpecker picked itself up and resumed its flight, apparently unharmed by the attack. The young woodpecker stayed away from the suet log for several days but did eventually return, to my great satisfaction.

I like to watch how birds behave and interact at the feeders outside my window. Observing how adult birds feed and teach their offspring to forage is a fascinating exercise. Crows, among the most intelligent of all birds, are an especially absorbing subject. Offspring born during one breeding season remain with their parents throughout the winter and then aid in the feeding of the next generation of chicks. I have watched an adult crow bring its two youngsters to the lawn of the OVLC in order to show them how to unearth peanuts buried by the squirrels. Watched closely by its offspring, the crow strutted about the lawn, searching, and within a few minutes, located and dug up a whole peanut. One could almost imagine the young crows having an 'aha' moment. In general the creatures at my feeding station get along quite well together and are reasonably companionable with a few conspicuous exceptions: if blue jays, starlings, or any of the squirrels are present, smaller birds will give way and remain a safe distance apart.

Despite the fact that Ottawa is located in a relatively northern location, we are privileged to have one hummingbird species — the ruby-throated — breed here each summer. Males have iridescent green backs, white underparts and fiery-red throats that flash like laser beams. Females have soft green backs and wings with white throats and breasts. Both sexes arrive in the Ottawa region in May. If, for some reason, they arrive before I have put out their feeder, they will fly impatiently about its usual location as if to ask, "Well, where is it?" Ruby-throated hummingbirds of both sexes are aggressive and not social. Apart from the brief time that males court females and consummate their relationship, the two sexes do not socialize. Once the female has been impregnated, she is left alone to build the exquisite, eggcup-sized nest and raise the offspring.

The nest is constructed largely of spider web and camouflaged with lichen. Not only does the spider webbing make excellent glue to hold the nest together, but it can also expand as the nestlings grow. A female will usually build her nest on top of a branch where it resembles a knot, thanks to the camouflage. She will then lay two tiny eggs and brood them herself until they hatch into naked, blind chicks. Hummingbirds feed on nectar and tiny insects; they are especially drawn to tubular flowers, which contain large amounts of nectar easily accessible with their thin, probing bills. They also find the colour red to be extremely attractive; for this reason, I have always planted some red-flowered plants in my garden bed. Whenever female hummingbirds nested on the grounds of the OVLC, their fledgling youngsters would come to my nectar feeders and to the flowers that I had planted underneath — red salvia, bee balm, red clover, cleome, gladioli and geraniums.

I am always intrigued to observe the behaviour of juvenile hummingbirds approaching my feeder for the first time. Although drawn by the colour red, not all the youngsters are able to determine that the centres of the red plastic flowers are a source of nectar. Some fly about aimlessly and then descend to the garden below to feed on real flowers. After repeated visits to the feeder, sometimes hovering and sometimes perching, these naïve youngsters eventually discover the feeding holes. One August I was surprised by two juveniles, possibly siblings, which spent a great deal of time playing together; ordinarily, these birds are aggressive toward each other. These two swooped in and out of trees, around the feeder, through the flowers, and up and down the side of the building. All young creatures love to play: it is an important activity for them as they learn to fly, maneuver, evade predators and improve their hunting skills.

As autumn progresses into October, hummingbirds begin to pass through the Ottawa region on their southward migration. In all my years of writing the bird column, I exhorted readers not to take down their hummingbird feeders at this time of year. It is a popular misconception that leaving them up will encourage the hummingbirds to linger and be killed by cold weather. Such is not the case — there is nothing stronger than the migration instinct. Furthermore, an abundant food supply at this time of year is crucial for these birds, as they must greatly increase their weight to fuel their lengthy migration. For many individuals this migration includes a non-stop, 800-kilometre crossing of the Gulf of Mexico to their wintering grounds in southern Mexico, Central America and South America.

· ·

Birds frequently preen their feathers to keep them in good condition for insulation and waterproofing. Most birds will bathe in birdbaths, puddles, fountains or other water sources to clean their feathers. Smaller birds, like warblers, vireos and kinglets, take baths among leaves made wet by rain or dew. In this way they are less exposed than they would be at a birdbath. One rainy day I observed a pileated woodpecker hanging on the trunk of a large tree in the forest, shaking its wings and fluttering its feathers. I realized after a moment of puzzlement that it was having a very good bath. Hummingbirds delight in flying through lawn sprinklers but will also use wet leaves in trees and shrubs to bathe. In contrast to most birds that prefer to bathe in water, some birds, like house sparrows, quail and turkeys, prefer to take vigorous baths in dust. The dust absorbs excess oil, which prevents feathers from becoming greasy or matted. It also helps to smother lice, feather mites or other parasites.

Birds were not the only creatures that visited my feeding station — over the years various animals dropped by as well. Not surprisingly the first animals that were attracted to my feeders were squirrels, mostly black ones at first, followed by native red squirrels, and finally, by a trio of grey squirrels. One of the greys was a beautiful male with the most magnificent, fluffy tail. The black squirrels destroyed the suet log feeders by chewing out the holes; they also detached the trays under the seed feeders so that the spillage fell to the ground rather than into the tray. I declared war on these mischievous creatures, aided by water guns and jets of water from the garden hose. It was to no avail. Despite my best efforts at preventing the squirrels from getting to the feeders, they always won. These pesky creatures appeared to have two mottos: 'Never give up!' and 'Keep coming back!' They seemed to understand that sooner or later I would have to leave the window. I was enthralled watching them strive to defeat every obstacle that I placed in their way. Eventually I put away the water guns, gave up the war and conceded defeat. I purchased a squirrel-proof feeder, which still allowed access for the smaller birds, such as chickadees, chipping sparrows, goldfinches and purple finches.

A large male raccoon caused me problems for several years. He lived in the forest but rummaged in the garbage bins of the OVLC at night. Sometimes the lids of these bins were left open, allowing him access to waste food on which he grew big and strong. He would often investigate my feeders on his nightly incursions. It was not unusual to find a feeder down on the ground, damaged or dragged away across the lawn. One night I was watching television in my room when I turned to see a spectacled face peering at me through the window. At first I feared that it was the return of this marauding male. With a sigh of relief I realized that it was just a young raccoon, barely tall enough to look in while standing on its hind legs. It returned for several nights, on one occasion delighting a nurse who had come to my room to give me some assistance.

Chipmunks are charming little animals — soft, brown, stripy and most precocious in their behaviour. Scampering about with their tails held erect, they spend the entire summer collecting and storing seeds and nuts for the winter. As soon as they fill their cheek pouches with seeds from my feeder, they rush off to store them and then come back for more. These friendly creatures do not hesitate to sit on my knee to accept a peanut offering. Chipmunks do have one most unfortunate activity — they delight in digging up my garden. The feisty creatures uproot newly planted annuals and leave them strewn on the ground; they also unearth and chew bulbs of lilies, crocuses and tulips. Their most dastardly crime was the destruction of an avocado seedling that I had managed to germinate. It was about five centimetres tall when I planted it outside for the summer. It did not survive its first night. In the morning I discovered the shoot lying on the ground, cut off from its large seed, which had been dug up and gnawed. I was very upset at the loss of my precious baby.

Chipmunks occasionally enter my room through the open window. They run around inside or sit on the table next to me. I give them peanuts in the shell, which they carry away three at a time — one in each cheek pouch, and one between their teeth. I once witnessed a demonstration of their intelligence. A chipmunk had successfully placed one peanut in a cheek pouch but discovered that the second peanut was too long. It took only a moment for the chipmunk to sit on the table, remove the shell of the peanut, and place the nuts in its other pouch. With both pouches full, it picked up the third peanut in its teeth and scurried away.

One winter three deer — a doe and two youngsters — came to feed at night. By craning their necks they reached a hanging seed feeder and licked it clean. They also slurped up whatever seed was scattered on the ground underneath the feeders. With their frequent visits they became quite tame. For several years red foxes maintained a den at the wild end of the OVLC property. On occasion an adult fox — a beautifully sleek animal — would run across the lawn or alongside the 'Great Wall of China'. The foxes successfully raised their family near Tony Princiotta Memorial Park, where a small pond was home to a family of exotic ducks. Unfortunately, the wily male fox discovered the ducks and systematically caught the ducklings until none remained.

These poor ducks had a difficult life — they were surrounded by predators. If they escaped the fox, they would often fall victim to the crows, which were notorious for stealing their eggs. The crows would eat the eggs on a bare patch of land above the septic field, leaving the area littered with pale shell fragments. The replacement of these exotic ducks with a flock of plain white ducks met with modest success: one new pair did manage to successfully hide and protect its nest so that six ducklings hatched. I feared that these fluffy little ducklings would fall victim to another local predator, a great blue heron, but their parents proved to be alert and protective. The family would form a tightly packed flotilla as they paddled around the pond with parent ducks positioned defensively, one fore and one aft. As a result of this excellent parenting, the young ducklings were able to grow up and fledge successfully.

I had a surprise visitor to my room one night. I had just come out of the bathroom in preparation for bed and went into the hallway to turn off the light. My eye was caught by what looked like a small lump of dirt near the door to my room. When I took a closer look, I discovered to my great surprise that it was a small toad! Clearly this creature would be more successful hunting out of doors than on my carpet, so I took it to the window and set it down in the garden beneath. With its ample protective cover the garden provided a safe home for the little toad. I spied it several times over the course of the summer. It must have hibernated somewhere in the garden for I saw it again in springtime and throughout the following summer.

Of course the '$64,000 question', which I discussed at length with staff and other residents, was, "How on earth did this amphibian get into my room?" My room is situated at the end of a long, carpeted hallway far from the nearest exterior door. My windowsill sits well above ground level, at a height that seemed too great for this small creature to leap. Several ideas were bandied about, none of which seemed plausible. Finally Claude Lafontaine, OVLC manager at the time, came up with the best explanation:

"It was," he said, "the frog prince looking for his princess."

We were all amused by this comment, and life went on with the toad a welcome addition to my family of wild creatures.

In 2013 I was pleasantly surprised to learn that I had been awarded the Queen's Jubilee Medal. Shortly after this award was publicized, Judy Tennant of Parrot Partner Canada contacted the OVLC and offered to put on a parrot demonstration as a tribute. Parrot Partner operates an education and adoption centre for the care and handling of parrots. The physical rehabilitation of parrots with behavioural or other problems resulting from abuse or neglect is one of their main activities. Once the birds are happy and healthy again, they are made available to new homes. The centre also counsels new and prospective owners about the needs of parrots and offers workshops on bird-human relationships. To adopt a parrot is a major commitment considering their long lifespan, which can be as much as 50 or 60 years.

Activity Directors Femmy Wright and Krissy Borutski accepted Judy Tennant's generous offer of a parrot show and decided to include a tea party for all the OVLC residents. Dietary Director John Russo kindly baked one of his festive cakes. On the appointed day Judy Tennant arrived with long-time volunteer Catherine Bromwell, a retired minister, and the event began. The first bird that Judy introduced was a handsome blue-and-gold macaw. These large, colourful birds are raucous and well known for their shrieking calls, which they often make while in flight. Each parrot was taken out of a travelling box and placed on its own perch facing the audience. The macaw did not think highly of its onlookers: it took one glance at us, immediately turned its back and remained in that position throughout the show. Judy told us about the macaw's history, where it came from, and its relationship with the other parrots. The second parrot to be introduced was a black-headed caique, also known as the 'seven-coloured parrot' because it has red eyes and feathers of white, black, blue, green, orange and yellow. It is a small, noisy bird native to the lowland jungle north of the Amazon River. Judy called this particular parrot 'a bully and a thug', adding that it was not popular with the other parrots in her facility. It made a regular nuisance of itself by chasing them about and creating a disturbance.

ELIZABETH WITH THE BLUE-AND-GOLD MACAW
PHOTO BY FEMMY WRIGHT

The pure white cockatoos were the last to perform. They could raise and lower their large crests at will; sometimes they synchronized these movements with their vocalizations. One of the birds, a Goffin cockatoo, had been taught to sing while the other, an umbrella cockatoo, had been taught to dance. The singer performed first — it had learned the lyrics 'Row, row, row your boat, gently down the stream.' The song continues 'Merrily, merrily, merrily, merrily, life is but a dream', but the cockatoo had not yet memorized those words. It would sing the first part and then stop. Judy asked the audience to supply the second part, which we were happy to do. And so it was that the OVLC seniors performed a duet with a Goffin cockatoo, much to the amusement of us all, including the cockatoo: it chuckled loudly when we concluded our singing. We repeated the song a number of times, and each time the cockatoo would follow our singing with a most enchanting, throaty chuckle. The dancing cockatoo used Judy's arm as its stage, moving nimbly up and down in time with the music. When the performance finished, Judy brought the parrot around to visit with members of the audience. The friendly umbrella cockatoo was happy to pace up and down our arms when offered the chance. The tea party followed with a cake that was both spectacular and delicious. A splendid afternoon was had by all!

Elizabeth's Fat Mix Recipe

1 cup melted suet, lard or fat from roasts and drippings (or purchased from your butcher)
1 cup chunky peanut butter
3 cups cornmeal
3 cups oats
Melt the fat and peanut butter in a large bowl. Add dry ingredients and mix well.
You can also add raisins, berries, chopped peanuts, other nuts and birdseed.
The mix can be put into a log that has widely staggered holes drilled in it so the birds do not rub their feathers on the fat. It can be formed into blocks for the cages that are available in bird shops or hardware stores.

Chapter 15:
MUSINGS OF A CENTENARIAN

· ·

As I consider what to write in this chapter, I have entered my hundredth year on this great planet. I have lived in an era of extraordinary change, a century that began with horse-drawn barges and finished with overwhelming advances in high technology. I have survived global wars and been privileged to live in two wonderful countries in which I could pursue my passionate interest in the natural world. The lovely sights that I have witnessed, the birding activities that I have enjoyed, the knowledge that I have gleaned — these have greatly enriched my life. And yet I have qualms that I wish to share.

During my time in Canada I have been struck by a number of unexpected and distressing facts. I have discovered to my chagrin that far too many Canadians cannot identify a sparrow or a starling; or distinguish between a robin and a crow. What I find even more disturbing is this: not only do these people not know basic facts, but they don't care to know. Many people have lived their entire lives without bothering to make any effort to discover and learn about the other magnificent life forms with which we share the planet — the animals, the birds and the flowers. I have met people who didn't know the difference between a tulip and a daffodil. I find this most distressing. Now that mankind has the technological power to change our environment so dramatically, for better or for worse, surely we have an even greater obligation to provide stewardship for the other living organisms with which we share the planet. To that end I am going to conclude this book with some specific suggestions as to what we might do to improve the lot of our avian friends.

Provide Food

A myriad of bird feeders are available today from commercial suppliers like wild bird shops, hardware stores and feed-and-seed outlets. Buy squirrel-proof feeders in the certain knowledge that your feeder will attract these cunning creatures. No squirrel-proof design is perfect, but some are better than others. Seek advice from staff as to which are the best. Tube feeders are cylinders fitted with openings and perches where a bird can sit and feed. These are generally easy to fill and clean.

There are a great many commercial seed mixes available in stores these days. You will have more success if you choose a higher quality mix that contains a greater variety of seed. (I was very gratified when my good friend Audrey Rooney of Rooney Feeds formulated an excellent blend of premium birdseed with my assistance and named it in my honour.) Cheaper mixes are often predominantly millet, which many birds do not like. Inexpensive formulations also tend to contain more seeds from weedy plants; these may germinate from scattered seed. Mixes with black oiled sunflower seeds are recommended over those with large, stripy sunflower seeds. Birds with less powerful beaks, like black-capped chickadees, can deal with oiled sunflower seeds but cannot break open the larger kind.

Niger seed is popular for members of the Finch family, such as American goldfinches, house finches and pine siskins. Because of the fine size of this black seed, feeding ports on niger feeders are quite small. Niger seed is expensive but can be mixed with finch seed, which is considerably cheaper. You can always add small amounts of niger seed to your other seed mixes too. Suet feeders are good for attracting woodpeckers, but unfortunately they will also attract European starlings.

When choosing a commercial feeder, look carefully at how easy it is to dismantle for refilling and cleaning. I have made several mistakes over the years by purchasing inexpensive feeders that proved to be far too fiddly in routine use. You will be better off in the long run to spend a little more money and buy a higher-quality feeder. Remember too that you must clean and sanitize feeders on a regular basis. Salmonella bacteria, spread by fecal matter, are a constant risk at busy feeders. Some species, like pine siskins, are especially vulnerable and can be killed by these bacteria. Clean your feeders regularly — I would suggest monthly. Scour the feeders clean with a bristle brush and then soak them for an hour in a dilute ten percent bleach solution, which will kill any salmonella present. Rinse thoroughly with fresh water, and dry completely before refilling.

Hummingbird feeders come in all sizes and shapes, some quite bewildering. Almost all of them will be red, the preferred colour to attract these charming birds. You may wish to buy more than one type and place them in different parts of your garden. Hummingbirds are renowned for their aggressive behaviour and will squabble for possession. While many feeders require hummingbirds to hover, others include perches where a bird can sit and feed quietly.

The standard sugar solution for hummingbirds is one part sucrose (ordinary white sugar) to four parts of water. It is preferable to boil and then cool this solution before use. Boiling will remove any chlorine in the water and kill any yeast or mold spores that might be present in the sugar. *Do not use honey, brown sugar, artificial sweetener or any red food colouring — just white sugar and water!* You may wish to prepare larger batches and store the excess in your refrigerator. Clean your feeder thoroughly at each refilling.

Don't Forget Water

Birds lack sweat glands and do not require as much water as mammals typically do. Nonetheless, they must replenish water lost through respiration and droppings. Insect-eaters need less water because some is replaced through their diet; on the other hand, seed-eaters require relatively more than other species. Natural water sources for birds include creeks, streams, ponds, rivers and lakes, where most birds will drink from the water's edge. A few species, like terns and swallows, may scoop water directly from the surface while lightweight birds, like warblers and vireos, may drink from the edge of a lily pad. Water droplets collected on leaves from rain or dew can also be a source of drinking water. In the home garden the nearest water source may be far away, so it is a good idea to make water available for birds. Birds are very attracted to the sound of running water. In addition to birdbaths, a small trickle fountain will prove to be a great draw for many species of birds, especially during migration or in times of drought.

Remember that birds also require water for bathing, which helps remove dust, dirt and parasites. Following a good bath, birds will preen thoroughly and rearrange their feathers. This distributes oil from their preen glands so that their feathers remain waterproof and trap layers of insulating air. Maintaining feather hygiene is especially important in winter when good insulation is needed to fend off the cold. My son Michael has told me about an overwintering Anna's hummingbird in his garden in Vancouver. That bird came faithfully to his fountain to bathe every morning in the pre-dawn gloom, even when the fountain was encrusted with ice and the air temperature was -8 °C.

Because birds will drink and bathe in the same water, you should change the water regularly. Be sure to scrub the birdbath to remove algae and debris. When possible I like to fill my birdbath with rainwater collected in barrels from the downpipes at Orchard View. If you use chlorinated tap water for your birdbath, let the water sit for at least a day to allow the chlorine to evaporate.

CREATE A BIRD-FRIENDLY GARDEN

Birds require shelter from the weather, from predators and for overnight roosting. If you want to attract more birds into your garden, plant trees and shrubs that provide good shelter. If those trees also offer potential food sources, so much the better. Evergreen conifers have thick branches with needles that offer year-round protection, and their cones contain seeds enjoyed by many birds. Shrubs with a dense, branching structure also provide excellent cover. Mountain ashes can be a little messy, but their fruit is sought after by thrushes, finches and waxwings. Other small-fruit trees that attract birds include crabapples, hawthorns, chokecherries and serviceberries.

If you have an ornamental garden that includes flowers and grasses, do not cut down seed-producing stems but leave them for the birds to forage in fall and winter. Scatter mulched leaves on flowerbeds to decompose by means of bacteria, fungi, snails and various insect larvae, all of which can provide a nutritious diet for birds that like to scratch in the soil.

ELIMINATE THE USE OF
PESTICIDES AND HERBICIDES

I am opposed to the cosmetic use of herbicides and pesticides in the home garden. I am a firm believer in good garden practices: effective soil management through regular applications of compost and manure; careful watering; removal of dead and diseased plant materials; and respecting the horticultural requirements of plants (shade-loving plants in the shade, sun-loving plants in the sun). If these basic principles are followed, then plants should develop strongly with good health and resistance to disease. With so many different plant materials available nowadays, it is a better strategy to replace a disease-prone plant with one that performs better rather than use a chemical treatment, which may well prove ineffective in any case.

Pesticides can kill birds both directly and indirectly. In the 1950s and 1960s, DDT did serious and widespread harm to the population of raptors, such as hawks, eagles and osprey. Not only does DDT kill birds directly by poisoning their nervous systems, it also interferes with their reproductive systems by causing thin eggshells and reducing hormones needed for egg laying. While DDT is now banned in Canada and the United States, it is still widely used in other parts of the world where it continues to have an impact on our migratory bird species. It is not just birds that are affected by the use of herbicides and pesticides. There is mounting evidence that other species, such as bees, wasps, butterflies and amphibians, are also adversely affected by their use.

PROVIDE PROTECTION

The principal killers of birds are cats, windows and power lines. Even if you don't own a cat, you can be certain that bird activity around a feeding station will attract the attention of neigh-bourhood cats. Cats rely on an element of surprise when they ambush birds. If your feeding station is in an open area, place it sufficiently high that a cat will have difficulty jumping onto it. This diminishes the likelihood of success for a stalking animal. If you own a cat, consider a bell for its neck, and keep it indoors as much as possible during migration season. Young birds unfa-miliar with the ways of cats are especially vulnerable during the fall migration. It is very difficult to keep cats out of one's garden, but a fence or chicken wire inside a hedge can make it difficult for them to enter without being noticed by the birds.

Windows are a hazard at any time of year but especially so in fall when many young birds on migration are unaware of the dangers of civilization. There are many actions that you can take to reduce the risk: install sheers, shutters, blinds or curtains, and close them at night so that birds are not attracted to the light within; move houseplants away from windows so that birds are not drawn to them; and place objects such as suncatchers, crystals, or silhouette cut-outs of hawks on the window as a visual deterrent. Many high-tech solutions are becoming available too. Search the Internet to see the full range of possible solutions.

BIRDWATCH WITH RESPECT

The first and most important rule for birdwatching is to keep your distance. In my career as bird columnist of the Ottawa *Citizen*, I had countless occasions to chat with birders filing viewing reports. One such conversation vividly illustrates how badly some birders can behave. A lady in the Ottawa area was very surprised to discover that she had a purple gallinule in her garden. Purple gallinules, also known as swamp hens, are large members of the Rail family. With purple breasts, olive-green backs, turquoise caps, large yellow feet and red beaks, purple gallinules are spectacular. They are native mostly to the coast-lines of the Caribbean Sea and are exceedingly rare in the Ottawa area. In general rails are shy and furtive birds, not easily seen. Perhaps this particular bird had been drawn to the large, well-cultivated garden maintained by my caller, for it provided ample cover and hence, protection.

When the identification of the purple gallinule was con-firmed, the lady in question kindly offered to allow birders onto her fenced property for viewings. She was keen that the birders maintain their distance because she did not want the gallinule frightened onto the neighbouring properties; these were rather barren by comparison and would expose the rail to the risk of predation. Almost immediately the poor lady regretted her gen-erous offer. She quickly discovered how difficult and uncaring some birders can be. In their haste to see the gallinule, and in some cases, get the best possible photograph, birders peered over her fence, trampled her garden, chased the gallinule about and flushed it out of her protective garden. The harassed bird was eventually captured and returned to a suitable habitat along the Florida coastline. In my final conversation with the lady, she expressed her disgust with the antics of the birders and vowed that should another rare bird visit her garden, she would never publicize it. How sad that some birders exhibited such poor behaviour, stressing both their generous hostess and the rare gallinule.

Birders in the Britannia woods recently caused serious stress to a pair of great horned owls by besieging their nest. Fluffy young owls leave the nest and come down to the ground before they are able to fly, leaving them especially vulnerable. It is very traumatic for them and their parents when they are confronted and frightened by large numbers of overly-close birders.

SNOWY OWL
PHOTO BY SAUL BOCIAN

It is not uncommon to have irruptions of northern raptors in winter when their food supply is periodically reduced by crashes in the lemming or mice populations. Hawk owls, snowy owls and great grey owls have all appeared in the Ottawa region in recent years, much to the delight of local birders. These birds often arrive in weakened condition, some close to starvation, and are further stressed by their unfamiliar environment. It has been very disappointing to see these beautiful creatures pestered by over-eager viewers and photographers approaching them far more closely than they should. With the powerful binoculars and camera lenses available nowadays, there is simply no excuse to harass these birds by getting too close. Surely we can do better! To that end the Ottawa Field-Naturalists' Club has developed and publicized a sensible and comprehensive list of dos and don'ts for birders. All those who watch or photograph birds should read and abide by their Code of Conduct.

EDUCATE OUR YOUTH

Canada is a vast country, blessed with wonderful natural splendour, including the last unbroken stretches of the great boreal forest that spans the globe. It is a cradle of life for many species of birds, including the warblers that migrate north each year to raise their families on the plentiful insect life there. We are fortunate that far-sighted politicians have established many federal, provincial and municipal parks over the years. This is a most worthy accomplishment, but in addition to protecting our existing parks, we must expand similar protection to other vital habitats, such as the boreal forest. Each generation — both present and future — must strive to maintain the quintessential integrity of the environment.

Parents, you have a great task ahead of you. Youth in this hi-tech age of computers, cellphones and social media are living in an entirely different world than their predecessors. Many of them live in an urban environment and are less and less aware of the natural world and all its inhabitants, of which they are but one. Please take the time to teach them about the remarkable diversity of living creatures that makes up the web of life. Instil in your children a love and reverence for this life. Only then will they have the knowledge and understanding that will ensure their commitment to preserve the remarkable legacy they have been bequeathed. Together we must make a sustained effort to halt the further degradation of the environment and preserve the habitat needed by our fellow travellers of the natural world — the animals, the birds, the flowers, the butterflies and other insects — for generations to come.

WHITE-CROWNED SPARROW
PHOTO BY JUDITH GUSTAFSSON

And Finally — Cherish our Fellow Species

In conclusion, I can do no better than cite the profoundly moving words of the great American naturalist, Henry Beston, first published in 1928:

> *"We need another and a wiser and perhaps a more mystical concept of animals. Remote from universal nature and living by complicated artifice, man in civilization surveys the creature through the glass of his knowledge and sees thereby a feather magnified and the whole image in distortion. We patronize them for their incompleteness, for their tragic fate for having taken form so far below ourselves. And therein do we err. For the animal shall not be measured by man. In a world older and more complete than ours, they move finished and complete, gifted with the extension of the senses we have lost or never attained, living by voices we shall never hear. They are not brethren, they are not underlings: they are other nations, caught with ourselves in the net of life and time, fellow prisoners of the splendour and travail of the earth."*

> – Henry Beston, *The Outermost House: A Year of Life on the Great Beach of Cape Cod*

Bird Lady
BIRD SPECIES: COMMON NAMES

. . . .

First Mention   Alphabetical

Chapter 1: My Early Years in Britain

First Mention	Alphabetical
Common cuckoo	Blue tit
Hedge sparrow	Common cuckoo
Mute swan	Common redstart
Eurasian kingfisher	Eurasian curlew
European stonechat	Eurasian kingfisher
Whinchat	European stonechat
Common redstart	Great blue heron
Great tit	Great tit
Blue tit	Hedge sparrow
Great blue heron	Mute swan

Chapter 2: The Second Great War

European robin	Blue tit
Blue tit	Chickadee
Chickadee	European robin
American redstart	American redstart
Common redstart	American robin
European robin	European robin
American robin	Common redstart
Yellow-billed cuckoo	Yellow-billed cuckoo
Ruby-throated hummingbird	Ruby-throated hummingbird

Chapter 4: Birding in the Ottawa Region

Baltimore oriole	Bald eagle
Rose-breasted grosbeak	Baltimore oriole
Indigo bunting	Black-crowned night heron
Scarlet tanager	Double-crested cormorant
Ruby-throated hummingbird	Eastern bluebird
Black-crowned night heron	Glaucous gull
Great horned owl	Great black-backed gull
Great blue heron	Great blue heron
Double-crested cormorant	Great egret
Great egret	Great horned owl
Bald eagle	Green heron
Red-winged blackbird	Herring gull
Sandhill crane	Horned lark
Lapland longspur	Iceland gull

Horned lark

Green heron

Herring gull

Ring-billed gull

Great black-backed gull

Lesser black-backed gull

Glaucous gull

Iceland gull

Eastern bluebird

Tree swallow

Purple martin

Indigo bunting

Lapland longspur

Lesser black-backed gull

Purple martin

Red-winged blackbird

Ring-billed gull

Rose-breasted grosbeak

Ruby-throated hummingbird

Sandhill crane

Scarlet tanager

Tree swallow

Chapter 5: Living beside the Rideau River

Pine grosbeak

Evening grosbeak

Pine siskin

Common redpoll

Purple finch

Hoary redpoll

Northern cardinal

Red-bellied woodpecker

Osprey

Bald eagle

Cooper's hawk

Sharp-shinned hawk

Great grey owl

American goldfinch

American robin

American woodcock

Bald eagle

Bobolink

Chipping sparrow

Common redpoll

Cooper's hawk

Eastern meadowlark

European starling

Evening grosbeak

Great blue heron

Great grey owl

. . . .

Hawk owl

Snowy owl

Rose-breasted grosbeak

American woodcock

Green heron

Great blue heron

Red-winged blackbird

American goldfinch

Eastern meadowlark

Bobolink

Snow bunting

Ovenbird

Tree swallow

House sparrow

Song sparrow

Chipping sparrow

American robin

Northern flicker

European starling

Green heron

Hawk owl

Hoary redpoll

House sparrow

Northern cardinal

Northern flicker

Osprey

Ovenbird

Pine grosbeak

Pine siskin

Purple finch

Red-bellied woodpecker

Red-winged blackbird

Rose-breasted grosbeak

Sharp-shinned hawk

Snow bunting

Snowy owl

Song sparrow

Tree swallow

Chapter 6: Raising Fledgling Birds

Ruby-throated hummingbird

Great horned owl

American robin

European starling

Green heron

Tree swallow

American goldfinch

American robin

Baltimore oriole

Barn swallow

Blue jay

Common nighthawk

Barn swallow

Purple martin

Eastern kingbird

Blue jay

Common nighthawk

Baltimore oriole

American goldfinch

House sparrow

Eastern kingbird

European starling

Great horned owl

Green heron

House sparrow

Purple martin

Ruby-throated hummingbird

Tree swallow

Chapter 7: Rattles the Kingfisher

Belted kingfisher

Belted kingfisher

Chapter 8: Joey the Pigeon

Rock dove (pigeon)

Tree swallow

Rock dove (pigeon)

Tree swallow

Chapter 9: Writing for the Ottawa *Citizen*

Red-winged blackbird

Common grackle

Brown-headed cowbird

European starling

Northern flicker

American goldfinch

Evening grosbeak

Penguin

Ivory-billed woodpecker

American goldfinch

Brown-headed cowbird

Chilean flamingo

Common grackle

European starling

Evening grosbeak

Ivory-billed woodpecker

Northern flicker

Penguin

Pileated woodpecker

Chilean flamingo

Yellow-nosed albatross

Pileated woodpecker

Red-winged blackbird

Yellow-nosed albatross

Chapter 10: Elisha the Flamingo

Northern gannet

Yellow-nosed albatross

Purple gallinule

Chilean flamingo

Chilean flamingo

Northern gannet

Purple gallinule

Yellow-nosed albatross

Chapter 11: Jacko the Parrot

African grey parrot

African grey parrot

Chapter 13: Birding Trips and Tours

South Africa

Limpkin

Knysna lourie
(Knysna turaco)

Southern red bishop

Red-winged blackbird

Knysna lourie
(Knysna turaco)

Secretary bird

Limpkin

Red-winged blackbird

Secretary bird

Southern red bishop

Trinidad and Tobago

Oilbird

Scarlet ibis

Tricoloured heron

Oilbird

Scarlet ibis

Tricoloured heron

. . . .

Costa Rica

Resplendent quetzal

Three-wattled bellbird

Bare-necked umbrellabird

White-throated magpie jay

Slate-throated redstart

Emerald toucanet

Chestnut-mandibled toucan

Slaty-tailed trogon

Red-capped manikin

Fiery-billed aracari

Boat-billed heron

King vulture

Bare-necked umbrellabird

Boat-billed heron

Chestnut-mandibled toucan

Emerald toucanet

Fiery-billed aracari

King vulture

Red-capped manikin

Resplendent quetzal

Slate-throated redstart

Slaty-tailed trogon

Three-wattled bellbird

White-throated magpie jay

Arizona

Phainopepla

Gambel's quail

Cactus wren

Blue-throated hummingbird

Acorn woodpecker

Mexican (formerly grey-breasted) jay

Audubon warbler

Ruby-crowned kinglet

Greater roadrunner

Yellow-headed blackbird

Brewer's blackbird

Abert's towhee

Acorn woodpecker

Audubon warbler

Black-shouldered kite

Blue-throated hummingbird

Brewer's blackbird

Broad-billed hummingbird

Cactus wren

Canyon wren

Gambel's quail

Gila woodpecker

Red-winged blackbird

Lark sparrow

Abert's towhee

Vermilion flycatcher

Scarlet tanager

Painted redstart

Canyon wren

Strickland's woodpecker

Hutton's vireo

Gila woodpecker

Scaled quail

Mourning dove

White-winged dove

White-crowned sparrow

Broad-billed hummingbird

Black-shouldered kite

Western bluebird

Pygmy nuthatch

Greater roadrunner

Hutton's vireo

Lark sparrow

Mexican (formerly grey-breasted) jay

Mourning dove

Painted redstart

Phainopepla

Pygmy nuthatch

Red-winged blackbird

Ruby-crowned kinglet

Scaled quail

Scarlet tanager

Strickland's woodpecker

Vermilion flycatcher

Western bluebird

White-crowned sparrow

White-winged dove

Yellow-headed blackbird

Britain

Eurasian stone-curlew

Garganey duck

Eurasian serin

Woodchat shrike

Black-necked grebe

Eider duck

Arctic tern

Aleutian tern

Atlantic puffin

Black grouse

Black-legged kittiwake

Black-necked grebe

. . . .

Great auk	Chough
Aleutian tern	Common greenshank
Lesser-crested tern	Corncrake
Sandwich tern	Dartford warbler
Arctic tern	Eider duck
Black-legged kittiwake	Eurasian serin
Northern gannet	Eurasian stone-curlew
European shag	European shag
Greater cormorant	Garganey duck
Atlantic puffin	Goldcrest
Common greenshank	Golden eagle
Golden plover	Golden plover
Black grouse	Golden-crowned kinglet
Slavonian grebe	Great auk
Grey wagtail	Greater cormorant
Ring ouzel	Grey wagtail
Peregrine falcon	Hawfinch
Golden eagle	Hen harrier
Corncrake	Lesser-crested tern
Wood warbler	Northern gannet
Goldcrest	Peregrine falcon
Golden-crowned kinglet	Red kite
Roseate tern	Ring ouzel
Chough	Roseate tern
Hen harrier	Sandwich tern
Red kite	Slavonian grebe
Dartford warbler	Willow tit

Woodlark

Hawfinch

Willow tit

Wood warbler

Woodchat shrike

Woodlark

Mexico

Painted bunting

Blue grosbeak

Sinaloa wren

Black-necked stilt

Crane hawk

Red-winged blackbird

Potoo

Mexican parrotlet

Russet-crowned motmot

Tufted jay

Bumblebee hummingbird

Bee hummingbird

Military macaw

Yellow grosbeak

Sparkling-tailed
hummingbird

Laughing falcon

Bee hummingbird

Black-necked stilt

Blue grosbeak

Bumblebee hummingbird

Crane hawk

Laughing falcon

Mexican parrotlet

Military macaw

Painted bunting

Potoo

Red-winged blackbird

Russet-crowned motmot

Sinaloa wren

Sparkling-tailed
hummingbird

Tufted jay

Yellow grosbeak

Grand Manan Island

Semipalmated sandpiper

Semipalmated plover

Bald eagle

Semipalmated plover

. . . .

Bald eagle   Semipalmated sandpiper

Chapter 14: Retirement at Orchard View Living Centre

Black-capped chickadee	American goldfinch
Hairy woodpecker	American robin
Downy woodpecker	Black-capped chickadee
Cooper's hawk	Black-headed caique
Common crow	Blue jay
American goldfinch	Chipping sparrow
Chipping sparrow	Cliff swallow
Eastern bluebird	Common crow
Tree swallow	Cooper's hawk
Pileated woodpecker	Downy woodpecker
Rose-breasted grosbeak	Eastern bluebird
White-breasted nuthatch	European starling
Red-breasted nuthatch	Goffin cockatoo
Blue jay	Great blue heron
White-winged crossbill	Hairy woodpecker
Red crossbill	House sparrow
Purple finch	Mourning dove
Mourning dove	Pileated woodpecker
Sharp-shinned hawk	Purple finch
American robin	Red crossbill
Cliff swallow	Red-breasted nuthatch
European starling	Rose-breasted grosbeak

. . . .

Wild turkey	Ruby-throated hummingbird
Ruby-throated hummingbird	Sharp-shinned hawk
House sparrow	Tree swallow
Great blue heron	Umbrella cockatoo
Black-headed caique	White-breasted nuthatch
Goffin cockatoo	White-winged crossbill
Umbrella cockatoo	Wild turkey

Chapter 15: Musings of a Centenarian

Black-capped chickadee	American goldfinch
American goldfinch	Black-capped chickadee
House finch	European starling
Pine siskin	Great grey owl
European starling	Great horned owl
Purple gallinule (swamp hen)	Hawk owl
Great horned owl	House finch
Hawk owl	Pine siskin
Snowy owl	Purple gallinule (swamp hen)
Great grey owl	Snowy owl

. . . .

Resources and References

Birds of Ecuador, Robert S. Ridgely and Paul J. Greenfield, Vol. II, Cornell University Press, 2001

Royal Society for the Protection of Birds, rspb.org.uk

Birdscope, Cornell Laboratory of Ornithology, Vol. 15, No. 3, 2001

Birding.uk.com

Humanesociety.org

Birdlife.org

Peterson Field Guide to the Birds of Eastern & Central North America, 6th Edition, Houghton Mifflin, 2010

All about Birds (allaboutbirds.org), Cornell Lab of Ornithology

The Outermost House, A Year of Life on the Great Beach of Cape Cod, Henry Beston, 1st Ed., Holt Publishing, 1928

Parrotpartner.com

Ottawa Field-Naturalists' Code of Conduct: http://www.ofnc. ca/birding/Code-of-Conduct.pdf).